DAVID BLACKBUR

Help!
It's Sunday

All-age worship
resource book

kevin mayhew

First published in 2004 by
KEVIN MAYHEW LTD
Buxhall, Stowmarket, Suffolk, 1P14 3BW
E-mail: info@kevinmayhewltd.com

KINGSGATE PUBLISHING INC
1000 Pannell Street, Suite G, Columbia, MO 65201
E-mail: sales@kingsgatepublishing.com

9 8 7 6 5 4 3 2 1 0

ISBN 1 84417 181 7
Catalogue Number 1500670

Cover design by Jonathan Stroulger
Edited by Graham Harris
Typesetting by Louise Selfe

Printed in Great Britain

Contents

About the author

David Blackburn was born in Coventry, and having studied English and American Studies at Hull University trained for teaching at Birmingham University. He returned to Coventry to teach English and worked in two schools there, becoming Head of English in one and a senior teacher in the other. He also taught Drama and Voice at a leading Midlands stage school, and produced musicals and wrote reviews for two local amateur operatic societies. He became a Reader in the Church of England in 1976.

He left teaching and trained for the ordained ministry at Trinity College Bristol; he served in churches in Bromsgrove and Halesowen and taught on the Worcester Diocese Reader Training course for four years. He is presently Rector of Kinver and Enville in Staffordshire. His hobbies include watercolour painting and writing musicals for schools. He is married to June, and they have three grown-up daughters.

Introduction

I have been doing all-age worship talks and school assemblies for what seems like a hundred years! The good thing is that I still have much to learn. There are, fortunately, many books and other resources now available to help the busy Christian teacher or minister to pull ideas off the peg, in the midst of a busy schedule, as well as what the Internet offers. Sometimes these resources have obviously been used and thoroughly tested. At other times, you wonder!

Some of the resources are very ambitious *(Give a bouquet of spring flowers, a pen, a map of Athens and a bus ticket to everyone in the congregation, etc.)* and some will suit your congregation, while others will not.

For me, a resource book works if I can look through all the detail and find an idea, or the germ of an idea that I can make my own and that I think will work with the people I lead.

This book is a sample of the talks I have devised over the last few years, all of which have been tried out, sometimes more than once, either in all-age worship services or in school assemblies.

You will notice that there are some original poems in this book. These poems happen to be part of my own style, but may not be part of yours! Do whatever you will with these materials, to stimulate, challenge and engage with the next generation.

DAVID BLACKBURN

Preparation and Presentation

Before you dive into the contents I would like to say a word about preparation and presentation. Here is my own checklist, and I hope you find it helpful.

- **No resource book has all the answers.** Be prepared to look at resources and use them in ways entirely different from the ones originally conceived by the author!

- **You *must* be well prepared. Start with prayer.** Then think through any moments in your talk that could go wrong . . . anticipate the answers your congregations might give and be ready, at a moment's notice, to drop everything and go in a different direction.

- **Bible stories, simply told and colourfully illustrated, make wonderful subjects for all-age worship!** You don't always have to be witty and inventive! Bible stories have the habit of being able to speak for themselves! However, the Bible is full of stories that are not quite as well known as Noah, Joseph and the birth of Jesus. It pays to delve into both Old and New Testaments – a rich storehouse of material.

- **Always have an aim to your talk.** Afterwards, reflect on whether the aim was achieved: with others, if possible, as well as with yourself.

- **Be clear and keep your language simple.** A member of one of my congregations, who had a very good honours degree, once said that she always got something out of my all-age worship talks because they were easy to understand. Don't be over-ambitious. This is theology on a stick, to some extent! However, it must have point and purpose, as well as integrity! Try to make one or two basic points, and to reiterate these, orally and visually, if possible.

- **Do make use of visuals.** Even if you are reading a poem, stick it inside a large, folded piece of coloured card and make the cover look interesting. People will pay more attention if you have bothered!

- **Make use of the sense of anticipation.** Nothing makes a group want to get to the presentation more than if someone is sitting at the front of church, stock-still, with a blanket over their head. In the same way, a table containing seemingly incongruous objects (all of which need to be big enough to be seen from the back) can also arouse curiosity. In a nutshell, whet people's appetites!

- **If using others to help you, rehearse them.** Similarly, if using puppets, work out how the puppet works beforehand. Decide on its voice and its mannerisms. Practise in front of a mirror or video – both are useful.

- **Get to know your props.** If you are using props make sure you know where they are, in what order you are going to use them, and how you are going to clear them away once the talk is over. Nothing is worse than a good talk being followed by ten minutes of clearing up. We are aiming for slickness. To that end, I once sat through a fascinating course led by James Jones, now Bishop of Liverpool. During one of the talks, he showed us several pieces of recorded TV and asked us to time the length of each shot or section. There are such things as *picture bites*, as well as *sound bites*, and you need to be aware of the concentration span of your congregation. People are used to a swift succession of things happening . . . so think about the dynamics, structure and delivery of the talk or presentation. There is a difference between being ponderous and being profound.

- **Make printouts of the highest quality.** Remember that children especially are used to computer-generated handouts, worksheets and wall-displays – in other words, resources of a very high quality. Scrappy bits of paper with the words *God, Love* and *Mercy* daubed on them in pale green crayon simply will not do any more. Make any banners or posters you want to use absolutely clear. Font size and style are important. Can your message be read from the back of the church? Check it out beforehand. Words written by hand on large sheets of card with broad felt tip often look better from a distance when highlighted with a yellow highlighter. Don't write words in capital or upper-case letters. Use both upper and lower case – this makes writing much easier to read, as does using sans serif fonts (fonts without curly bits!). Visual resources *must* be as professional as you can make them. Often, the visuals are what the congregation remembers a month later! If your church has PowerPoint, Publisher or an equivalent, use these to produce handouts and overhead transparencies.

- **Puppets have a key role.** These can be invaluable as foil characters, staters of the obvious or askers of the difficult or most obvious question, etc. So much the better if the puppet can be a character who is 'hot' at the time of your presentation. The problem, often, is that although the manufacturers make soft toys or plastic versions of characters on TV they rarely make puppets. I wanted a puppet version of *Bob the Builder,* and it had to be seen from the back of church. Our local toy megastore had only hand puppets of *Sooty* and two wimpish-looking characters from *The Wind in the Willows.* However, the shop *did* sell a pyjama-case version of my chosen character, and also a child's back-pack version. I opted for the back-pack, and with some judicious snipping off of shoulder straps, had just what I was looking for! Remember, there is always more than one way of doing it! Choose puppets with which your congregations, and especially the youngsters, can identify. They are wonderful leaders-in!

- **Check out the sound system.** If one is available, do a sound-check beforehand. If you are thinking of involving children speaking, or intend interviewing children, a hand-held microphone is essential.

- **Gather the younger children and those of primary school age around you at the front.** They can sit on hassocks, if they are available. When they are sitting under your nose, you can use them as resources, get them to stand up and hold things, and control them quite well. Incidentally, it is a good thing to announce near the beginning of the service that parents of very young children must not feel obliged to keep the youngsters tied to the pews if they get fractious. Tell them to take the children for a walk round if they get cross. The parents of very small children need to know that they and their offspring are welcome, that you would rather have them in church making a noise than at home making a noise! Have a good selection of children's books and toys ready at the back of church for those children who cannot actually cope with the service, or organise a crèche for the babies and toddlers.

- **Get to know the children.** It doesn't hurt to 'interview' a few children before the talk starts – they are important, and it helps other church members to get to know them. You can also do this with adults. Also, when there are two small children in a family and they are with you at the front of church, a good question to start with is: 'Which of you is the noisy one, and which is the quiet one?' This always works for me! What else should you ask them? How old? Brothers and sisters? Are you married(!!) Which school do you go to? Teacher's name? Favourite lesson or food, etc. It is important physically to stoop down and be on the same level as the child, by the way!

- **Involve yourself in the talk.** 'On the way to church this morning, I saw . . . what do you think?' Otherwise, it can get a bit clinical. As I've already said, be ready to involve the children in your talks . . . either by asking them questions or by getting them to hold things, etc.

- **Have fun, and try to be relaxed.** Occasionally it is a good idea (though a daunting one) to have your talk videotaped. It's surprising what funny little habits we can develop without realising.

- **Your talk *must* have a clear and definite ending.** The congregation or assembly must be able to remember the gist of it a week later.

- **Remember to let in God!** We are not there simply to tell stories with morals or to make ethical points. We are there for God's sake. Even if there is a distinct turn-off from your talk the moment you mention Jesus, in schools, for example, mention him you should! Take, for instance, the Presentation on *Personal Alarms*. If you are using this material in a primary school that doesn't have any particular church affiliation, you might decide to leave out the section that deals with Peter. But you would not do so, I hope, if using the same talk in church. One more point regarding schools: It is considered good practice, when taking school assemblies, to leave your audience with something to think about and talk about when they get back to their classrooms. Always try to leave them with questions about what you've said, which are appropriate to the Key Stage they have reached. If working in a primary school with KS1 and KS2, your question for the Reception age group is going to be different from your question for Year 6. OFSTED inspectors will be looking for these questions!

- **Your voice is of paramount importance.** Is it dull, drab and monotonous *(Thus Uz the Bur Bur Sur Hurm Survurs)* or are you making the right use of pitch, pace, power of your voice, pause, inflection and diction? The voice needs working on. It is like a radio carrier wave – it is the main means of conveying your message. As for the art of reading aloud – did you know that reading aloud can make or break an otherwise good presentation? Hold the book to the side; go slowly enough to be able to lift your eyes from the page and engage the audience with your eyes; don't hurry . . . if you go about a third of the speed that seems natural, you'll be reading at the right speed. Vary the speed, of course, and use all the things talked about above. Above all, use the full vocal range! It is a natural tendency of the human voice to rise as the sentence reaches its end. So begin a new sentence at the deep end rather than at the top of the vocal range, otherwise you will have problems! Read whatever it is as if it has never been read before . . . and practise in front of a mirror! Those who are not used to reading aloud often make the following basic mistakes:

  - Reading in a monotone or without due care of the sense. Remember that English is a *colloidal* language: it flows from one vocal emphasis to another, like the waves of the sea – unlike French, which is monosyllabic.
  - Dropping the voice at the ends of phrases and sentences.
  - Gabbling.
  - Not taking in the sense of a phrase or sentence before actually reading it aloud. Not being *aware* of the sense!
  - Shouting.
  - Being too quiet.

  NB: If children are to read aloud, they must be well rehearsed. Above all, they must be loud enough, without bellowing!

- **How will I know that it is going well?** People will all actually be listening to you, and attending to what you are saying. You will have a real feeling of holding them in the palm of your hand, for God's sake. This is a rare privilege, and we must not abuse it! It is also a very good idea to reflect with others about how well something has gone.

The point is that we must be professional, accessible, we must have a message that we believe in, must make the talk our own, feed everyone in the congregation, and we must give God a chance to be heard! Now read on!

The Story of Wild Eagle

Summary   A traditional tale retold. Use at the beginning of a new school year, or adapt the talk for a baptism service.

Aim   To show that when God promises he will never leave us or forsake us, he actually means it!

Materials
- Copy of story, stuck onto a piece of card in the shape of an Indian tepee.
- Indian headdress to wear, or to use to whet their appetite.
- If you want to do some follow-up work on this (e.g., if the children are going out after your talk), you could have a large cardboard totem pole already pinned up in the venue. Children illustrate parts of the story, and these are stuck on the totem pole at the end of the service.

Readings   Psalm 23 (God is always with us, whether we are in joy or in darkness); 1 Samuel 12:22; Isaiah 41:17. Story of the Good Samaritan, if appropriate to context.

Presentation

This is a good session for the start of a new term, so it's appropriate to ask who has moved school or moved class. Talk about experiences – nice teachers, any new things or routines, new friends? Engage with older members of the congregation by asking who can remember going to school for the first time, moving into a new class or changing schools?

Here's a story about a boy who had to make a new beginning, who came to an important stepping stone in his life.

Many moons ago, when native Americans still lived freely in their territory, there were many tribes. There were the Ojibwa, Sioux, Iroquois and Shawnee; the Pawnee and the Mohawk. And in the forests where the Oneida tribe lived, there was a great chief. Brave and fierce, he was feared by his enemies and respected by everyone as a noble and fearless warrior. His name was Hawkeye. He had many sons and daughters.

Hawkeye's youngest son was called Wild Eagle. He was 12 years old, and although strong and brave, he *was* still a child. One day Hawkeye called Wild Eagle to his tent; he put his strong hand on the child's shoulder.

'Wild Eagle, my son,' said the great chief, 'it is time for you to undergo the test to see whether you are ready to take your place amongst the other braves of our tribe. You must come with me at dawn tomorrow morning into the great forest. You must bring food only for one day, and your bow and arrow and knife.'

Wild Eagle was both excited and terrified by what his father told him. He was very anxious to take his place in the tribe, but he was afraid because he did not know what the test would involve.

The next morning he and his father left the shelter of the camp, and walked into the great forest. They did not stop for rest all day, except to drink at noon from a fast-running stream, and to eat some hominy bread, which they carried in their pouches. As the sun was beginning to fade and it grew dark, the boy became tired and they stopped in a small clearing. The great chief spoke.

'Wild Eagle, the test you must undergo is to stay here in the middle of the forest all night. You may have no fire . . . no food . . . no shelter . . . only your knife and your bow and arrow. I shall return for you when the sun rises in the morning.'

The boy said: 'What if I am attacked in the night, Father, by tribesmen from another village . . . or owls . . . or wolves . . . or even the great black bear who lives in this forest?'

'That is part of the test, my son,' said the chief. 'Now I must leave you.'

When his father had gone, the boy curled up inside his blanket, and tried to get to sleep . . .

He was awoken sometime later by the howl of a wolf. He sat up, and an owl flew past his ears. The boy was terrified. It was snowing, and he was all alone, miles from anywhere . . . at the mercy of who knows what? His heart gave a leap, as in the shadows he thought he could see something moving. But he was afraid and dared not go and look. Then he heard a sound which turned his blood to ice . . . the roaring of the great black bear! It drew nearer and nearer. A wave of panic, like hot fire, swept over the boy. If only his father were here . . . *He* would save him.

The glassy moon rose high above the trees. The roaring stopped as suddenly as it had started; and the boy fell into a deep and lonely sleep.

He awoke at dawn, when the birds began to sing. He sat up with a shock. There at his side was a blazing fire . . . and covering his body was a warm blanket made out of the hair of a bison. Suddenly there was a stirring in the trees, and his father came striding out into the clearing to meet him.

The boy told him how frightened he had been. He told him about the roaring noise, and the fact that he thought he had seen something moving in the darkness of the forest . . . and how he had woken up in the morning to find the fire blazing, and the blanket covering his body.

'Have you not guessed what happened?' asked his father. 'It was me moving in the forest during the night. It was me who lit the fire while you were asleep, and I also placed the blanket over you. I have been over there behind that great oak tree all night long. I have never left you, or taken my eyes off you. I saw you when the bear came close. I would not have left you here alone and unprotected all night long. No . . . I care for you so much, and I would not have a hair on your head hurt. Come, have some breakfast. You have passed the test.'

After they had eaten, Wild Eagle and his father went home together. And it's a very strange thing . . . but the boy was never again afraid of being in the woods alone . . . because he knew he was *not* alone. There were owls . . . and wolves . . . and great black bears . . . and there was also . . . his father.

Consolidation

Talk about the fears the boy had . . . and the fact that he wasn't alone after all. Reflect that even when we are afraid, or facing something new, if we ask God to be with us he will be with us. He loves us so much. He has counted all the hairs on our head, and he loved us so much that he gave us the most precious thing he possessed . . . Jesus.

Our response

- Thank him and praise him.

- Pray to him so that we can know his will for us.

- Even when we are afraid or alone, we know God still loves us and cares for us.

- Show God's love and care to others, as he shows them to us.

- Explore the phrase, 'to be there' for someone. What does it mean? Give examples of how you have been there for someone, or someone has been there for you. Compare it with the fact that God is with all who love him.

Prayer

Father God,

we thank you that before we loved you, you loved us.

Thank you that you are never far away.

Help us to call out to you and to feel your presence with us.

May we take your love, strength and kindness

with us into the week ahead.

Amen.

The Two Trees

Summary   For use at Harvest or a Baptism

Aim   To be aware that spiritual nurture is as important as physical nurture.

Materials

- Gardening clothes, watering can, trowel, bottle of fertiliser, gardening gloves.
- Tree in a container (it could be artificial).
- On the tree: several pieces of 'fruit' which are in fact inflated balloons, each containing a written message. Messages are: *don't forget to share; love one another; shine God's light in the world; God loves a cheerful giver; help one another; make friends, not enemies; prayer changes things; do not pay back evil for evil.*
- A dead piece of a tree, stuck into a plant pot.
- Copies of script.

Presentation

Beforehand, nominate a member of the congregation to act the part of X. He* is out of sight as the Presentation begins. All through the service, the tree with the balloons on it, and the dead tree, have occupied prominent positions, and whenever possible, those taking part have admired the tree with the balloons, but looked with distaste upon the dead tree in the pot.

Leader Now, where is X? He disappeared earlier . . . I wonder where he could have gone. Let's call for him. Let's all shout: 'Where's X?', after three . . . are you ready? ONE – TWO – THREE!

Congregation Where's X?

(X suddenly appears, dressed as a GARDENER, from the back of the building, carrying a watering can, trowel, bottle of fertiliser, and wearing the gardening gloves.)

X Sorry to leave the service so suddenly, earlier on . . . I thought I would bring a tree I've grown to the service . . . it's there, look, at the front. I thought the children might like to have a go at picking the fruit. But I noticed the tree was looking a bit thirsty, so I decided to go round the back and get a watering can so it could have a really good drink. Have you missed me?

Leader Of course we have. Some of us were getting quite worried about you! Can we have a proper look at this tree of yours?

X Yes . . . what about the children? Would they like to come and look at it?

(Leader and X gather up as many children as possible and they all go to admire the tree bearing the balloons.)

---

* The part of X can be played by either sex.

Leader It's a magnificent tree, isn't it, children? And look at all that fruit. My goodness, X, it must have taken you a great deal of love and patience and kindness, and tender loving care to get the fruit so ripe.

X As a matter of fact, somebody gave it to me as a seedling a few Christmases ago. I've spent ever such a lot of time on it . . . you know . . . watering it . . . talking to it. I'm rather pleased with the way it's turned out. And do you know, the fruit is very special.

Leader Well I had noticed the fruit did look a bit . . . a bit different.

X Yes they are. . . for one thing, there's something inside each piece of fruit on the tree.

Leader Is it something to eat? A Mars bar, or a packet of Doritos?

X Something much more special than that. Inside each one is a special message.

(The children are invited to pop the balloons and read out the messages inside.)

Leader Congratulations, X! You've looked after this tree so well that it's produced some wonderful fruit, and the messages can really help us live our lives as God wants us to live them. Now, I'm afraid I have a confession to make. Do you see this? *(He picks up the other 'tree')* Somebody gave me this tree for my last birthday . . . but I forgot all about it . . . and now it's all dried up, and dead, and useless . . .

X I suppose you could burn it.

Leader That's about all it's fit for.

Consolidation

This story of our two trees is an important one at Harvest or at a Baptism. It has something special to say to all the mums and dads. God wants us to grow just like X's tree . . . so that we can produce fruit that will allow us to be more like God wants us to be. It's all up to our parents to be like the gardener, and tend the tree well, and nurture it. And it's also the job of the church family.

Everybody knows that if you don't introduce children to food and water at a very early age, they die, physically. But perhaps what we sometimes forget, is that unless we feed our children spiritually, from a very early age, they will shrivel up and die very quickly, from a spiritual point of view. So the story of these two trees is a challenge for all the adults.

Prayer

Father,

at this Harvest time / Baptism,

we thank you for the gift of children.

Help us to care for their physical

as well as their spiritual well-being.

Help all the members of the church

to encourage families to grow in Jesus,

and give us all the gifts of your Holy Spirit,

so that we may be more like the people you want us to be.

Amen.

God with Us

Summary   For use in Advent

Aim   To consider the importance of prayer as we engage with

God . . . as well as to consider its uses and abuses!

Materials
- Copies of the script.
- A portable battery-operated radio.

Presentation

I'd like to make a list, with your help, of the people we come into contact with each day. *(Especially engage with the children at this point, and draw upon the adults only if necessary. If there is an overhead projector or flip chart, someone could write the contacts down)* Ask who could cope with being on their own on a desert island for any length of time. Most people need the company of others. Why might this be so?

(Talk about someone you saw last week, living alone, who didn't have any visitors all week. How do you think this person felt?)

There are lots of visitors here this morning. Some are making music, others are talking, some are speaking in foreign languages! Listen. Can you hear them? *(Silence)* No? That's probably because we need something to enable us to hear them. *(Produce radio: turn on and move dial round)* Can you hear them now? Good!

God wants to talk to us and be with us every day . . . even when we are like the person I mentioned earlier who never gets any human visitors. Even the person stranded for years on a desert island or locked in solitary confinement in a prison cell can be in constant touch with God. How can we hear what he is trying to say to us? Could we use the radio, do you think? What about the Internet?

(Ask the congregation for ideas; be ready for a few bizarre answers from little ones! Help them, eventually, to get to the word – Prayer.)

Prayer

Prayer is our way of allowing God to be with us: to have a talk with us. Have you ever tried it? Some people spend hours every day doing it. Others only have a few minutes in the car on their way to work. Most of us find prayer quite difficult. But you know, and it's rather sad to say it, sometimes our prayers don't actually allow God to be with us at all. Have a listen to this! . . .

Voice 1   Hello, God! Now, I've only got a minute or two, so I hope you're listening . . . OK . . . Now then, have you got a pencil or a clay tablet and a chisel ready, or something? Because I warn you, this is a pretty long list.

Summer holidays first: I think the south of France would be nice next year, don't you? We could do with a bit of sunshine after that disaster you arranged for us last year at Ilfracombe. It rained for the whole fortnight, remember? Then there's the car. We'd like a nice new one, please, if you can arrange it . . . by the end of January would be nice. Now there's the little matter of my job. Well, I'm sorry, but it's totally boring. Can you fix me up with something different . . . say by Thursday? Better paid, of course, and nearer home if you could manage it. Then there's the new house. We're a bit disappointed about that, if I'm honest with you. You could have definitely done better, if you want my frank opinion. We've had our place on the market for more than six months now, and nobody's been to look at it yet. You know, sometimes I wonder if you ever listen to a single word I say . . .

Voice 2   Hello . . . it's me again, God. Got rather a long list for you today, I'm afraid. First there's the lady next door. She's been having those bad headaches again recently. Could you do something for her, do you think? Then there's Uncle Fred. Gone into hospital, he has. Not at all well. In fact, proper poorly! Do you think you could sort him out? Pardon? Me? Oh, I'm all right . . . I suppose. A bit worried about being made redundant, if I'm truthful . . . and I haven't been sleeping very well . . . but you don't want to hear about me . . . I don't mind praying for others . . . but I feel very selfish trying to pray for myself . . .

Voice 3   What? Pray? Me? Not likely! Tried it once. Never worked, did it? It's a waste of time and effort!

24

Voice 4   Hello again, God . . . now before you say anything, I must just tell you what happened this afternoon. I was coming home in the car, you see, and I was listening to the radio. Radio 1 it was . . . or perhaps it was Radio 2 . . . do you know, I can't remember. Anyway, there I was, on the Anytown* Road . . . you know, the dual carriageway . . . it's very busy at this time of year, but I prefer it to the other way . . . you know . . . the one that cuts round the back of all the shops and factories. Anyway, I was going along the Anytown Road, doing about 35-40, though I wasn't really watching the clock . . . it's never worked properly since it came back from the garage after its last service. Wasn't the only thing wrong with it when it came back, either. I swear there's this funny knocking sound under the bonnet when it's in third gear. I don't think I'll take it there again. My cousin takes hers to this new place that's just opened in New Town.* Quite cheap, she said it was, too. *(Pause)* Now then . . . where was I . . .?

---

* Localise these references

Consolidation

Like the voices and the music on the radio, God is with us all the time. The problem is we sometimes don't really take much notice of him. But most of all, we don't allow him to be with us because we just don't listen.

Let's all use this time before Christmas to remember God's promise that he wants to be with us all the time through his Son, Jesus. And as we think of that, let's do a bit more listening to what he is saying to us.

Voice 5   If you do not stand firm in your faith, you will not stand at all. The Lord himself will give you a sign. The virgin will be with child and will give birth to a son, and will call him Emmanuel: God with us.

Prayer

Father God,

we thank you that through prayer

we need never be on our own.

We can always use prayer to talk to you

and hear what you want to say to us.

Teach us how to pray, and give us the gift

of being able to listen to what you are saying.

Amen.

Christmas (1)

Summary

A virgin will conceive and bear a son, and he shall be called Emmanuel, a name which means God with us.

Aim

To reflect on the fact that the presents we give each other at Christmas do not last. The present God gave to the world at Christmas is for each one of us individually, if we will accept it. That present is constant and never wears out – it is Jesus.

Materials

- Before the service starts, have a table placed in a prominent position.
- On the table is a large cardboard box, covered with Christmas wrapping paper and tinsel, etc.
- Inside the box:

    One used tie: hideously out of fashion: from the 'flower-power' or 'kipper tie' era.

    One old tie or scarf: can be fairly modern, but holes have been cut in it.

    One empty bottle of wine.

    One empty box of chocolates.

    A copy of a novel.

    Old theatre ticket or cinema ticket.

(Feel free to ring the changes with this list, or to delete items or add new ones. Substitute scarves, hats or handbags for ties. If handbag, make sure the handle or zip is broken.)

Presentation

(Assuming use of list as written above.)

Isn't it strange that at Christmas, which is Jesus' birthday, we actually give presents to one another, and not to Jesus himself? Last year I had lots of presents . . . and the year before that . . . and the year before that . . .

(Taking out ancient tie) Here's a tie I got back in *(state year)*. It was given to me by my first girlfriend for my birthday.* I wore it every day back in *(state year)*. Wouldn't wear it now, though. *(Engage with congregation or audience as to why not. Be careful not to dismiss out of hand any unexpected or wacky answers. Get to the main idea that the tie is old-fashioned, and that you wouldn't be seen dead in it. If desired, have a volunteer out at the front, and put the tie round his neck. Banter with volunteer and audience about what it looks like.)*

(Box of chocolates) Hmmm! These were lovely chocolates *(to volunteer 2)*. Want one? Well you can't have one, I'm afraid *(when volunteer says yes)*, because they were all eaten on Christmas day. Wouldn't it be marvellous if somebody invented a box of chocolates that never emptied itself?

(Ask what might have been inside the bottle . . . tease the congregation, perhaps, and say you think it might have contained perfume . . . milk . . . petrol! Own up to the fact that it was wine, and that it tasted wonderful.) Trouble is . . . the wine has now been drunk, and the only thing to do with the bottle is to have it recycled.

(Copy of novel) My aunt gave it to me. I know she sent it to me because my dad sent it to her last year. She has read it, so now she's passing it on. *(Or you could say)* It was a novel I really wanted and I have now read it three times.*

In any event, I won't be reading it again . . . until I retire perhaps! So it will sit on my shelf and gather dust . . .

(Tie/scarf with holes) I am so upset about this; it's my favourite tie/scarf and it's got the moth!

(Theatre/cinema ticket) Do you know what it is? My mother bought it for me. I really enjoyed the outing. Trouble is . . . I've used the ticket up, and the performance is over.*

---

* Substitute people and occasions as you wish.

Consolidation

The common factor with these things is that they don't last. They come to the end of their lives by one means or another. All the presents we give each other are bound to come to the end of their lives or wear out.

God gave the world a present at Christmas . . . what was that present? The Bible tells us, and experience shows us that if we accept God's present of Jesus, he will never fail us, leave us or wear out. He is constant and never lets us down.

But do we want to accept this present? Do we feel we have a need to accept it?

Twenty years ago, Mrs White received a present from her sister Rachel. It was a pair of cheap, plastic 'pearl' earrings. It was all Rachel could afford. Mrs White was very upset to receive such a cheap and shoddy present, and she threw the earrings onto the back of the coal fire where they instantly fizzled away to smoke.

She was embarrassed by the present, and felt no need for it.

Some people are embarrassed by the name of Jesus.

Some people feel no need for him.

Jesus is the most constant, most precious gift any of us will or can ever receive. This gift is not forced on us. We have to reach out and ask for it. We can take it with us on our journey of life, or throw it on the back of the fire. The choice is ours and ours alone.

Prayer

Father God,

we thank you that you took the risk of sending Jesus

into the world on that first Christmas Day.

Help us to accept him,

to get to know him more each day, and to trust him.

May he have a place in our thoughts this Christmas,

and help us to take him with us into the rest of our lives.

We ask this in Jesus' name.

Amen.

Christmas (2)

Summary

This talk was the idea of the late Revd Martin Hunt, Christchurch, Southport, and it helps us to focus on Jesus, not just Christmas.

Aim

To remind the target group that the Bible says that Jesus came into the world as king; that he fights for us in a dark world; and that he is the light of the world, and in him there is no darkness at all.

Materials

- Large Christmas cracker made of three tubes of A3 card, red crêpe paper, silver paper, silver tinsel, etc. It must look as professional as possible, and must be easily visible from the back of the building. Either have it on display in a prominent place throughout the service or assembly, or cover it up, so that people wonder what it is.
- Three presents inside the cracker, wrapped in Christmassy paper – torch, toy sword, crown.

Presentation

Engage with the audience or congregation . . . either move amongst them, asking what they would like for Christmas, or if after the event, what they got for Christmas, OR arrange for three young volunteers to come out and help you pull the cracker, and ask them. If the talk is being given on Christmas Day or on the Sunday after, this is the moment to ask the children to show you what they got. Several of them will have invariably brought their Christmas gifts with them to church.

Christmas Crackers: Talk about them: Who likes them? Who doesn't like the bang? When do you have them? What do they have in them? etc.

Christmas crackers were invented in the late nineteenth century by an enterprising English baker, Tom Smith, who, by 1900, was selling 13 million worldwide each year.

Introduce the cracker, and thank those who made it, unless it was you! Get the volunteers to help you pull the cracker. Make a big fuss with this, getting the congregation to count: *'One, two, three, go!'* or do something similar that adds to the fun.

Get the volunteers to open each present in turn.

- Crown: Jesus came into the world as King. What does a king do? What powers does he have? What special qualities did Jesus have, and still has, today? Make it as simple or as complex as you think the target group can cope with.

- Sword: Because Jesus has overcome sin and death and everything evil, he has the power to fight everything that wants to hurt us. When we put our trust in him, he uses his sword to defend us in all circumstances.

- Torch: This reminds us that in John's Gospel, Jesus told his friends that he is the Light of the world – in him there is no darkness at all. Explain the implications of this. When we are in the dark, we are afraid. When I was a child, I couldn't sleep unless the light was on. I was afraid of the dark. There is much darkness in our world, so we need to live with the light on, a light that casts no shadows – that light is Jesus.

Consolidation

This will depend on the slant of your talk and the degree of its sophistication. You want people to take the images of the Crown, Sword and Torch with them into the world. Have the children hold each one up in turn, and ask for volunteers in the congregation to remind us all of what the symbolic value is of each object. Reiterate that they remind us of the *strength* and *power* of Jesus, and that he fights for us.

Prayer

Dear Father God,

we thank you for Christmas, and especially for today's

reminder that Jesus is the King of the universe;

that he wants to fight for us;

and that he shines like a bright beacon in a world

that is so often dark and sad.

Help us to be his people, and to take his light with

us into our daily lives.

In his name we pray.

Amen.

Christmas (3)

Summary

For use when reflecting on gifts – and the Gift!

Aim

To discover for the first time, or to be reminded, that Jesus came into the world not as a knight in shining armour, but in great humility.

Materials

- Either a small Christmas tree on a table with three presents (as described later) underneath it, or . . .
- A large cardboard box wrapped in Christmassy paper with tinsel etc., containing three presents:

  1. An enormous box, wrapped in sumptuous Christmas paper, with all the trimmings. Inside it are three or four other boxes and packets, each inside the other, in the same way that Russian dolls fit together.

  2. Another beautifully wrapped box, preferably an empty biscuit tin or chocolate box. Emphasis on empty!

  3. A box of chocolates or a bar of chocolate, wrapped hastily in newspaper and bits of string. It MUST look tatty and uninviting!

As in other talks, it is important to maintain eye contact with the volunteer and to engross her/his imagination. Have the objects at the front on a table. Maybe cover them at the start of the assembly or service, and then remove the cover during a hymn or song. Anything that whets the appetite . . .!

Note: it is important, when choosing volunteers, to pick children who are still more or less at the concrete thinking stage. Infants, and especially Reception Class infants, make ideal subjects for this one! Choose anyone older, and they might work things out for themselves, and the talk turns to stone! I had a curate, once, to whom this happened . . . *Caveat emptor!*

Presentation

Select three volunteers: Who would like to come and a) open these presents under the Christmas tree – Have you got a tree? Where is it kept? Has it got lights . . .? Who decorated it . . .? etc., *or* b) see what's in this box?

(Assuming we are dealing with the box) I wonder what this box is doing here . . . any ideas? *(Collect and discuss ideas from the volunteers and congregation in general. It is often a good idea in any talk in which you are engaging with children, to have a few well-primed adults in the congregation who can chip in and show that they are involved, or else help you out of a tight situation!)*

One by one, the volunteers each choose a present from the box. If you have done your homework, and selected the right children, the enormous present will go first; then the other nicely presented one; and finally, and rather grudgingly, the tatty parcel will be chosen last.

The first Christmas box is gradually opened. There is one box inside another, but in the final box there is a note saying 'Sorry, nothing doing'.

Secondly, open the beautifully wrapped box. The point, here, is that even though the box is nicely wrapped, it contains absolutely nothing.

The tatty parcel is opened, and reveals a big bar of chocolate!

Consolidation

This is where we have the privilege and the challenge of talking about what Paul calls *the paradox of God*. You could refer to 1 Corinthians 1 – it will depend on your congregation. Bring out the reasons why God chose to send Jesus into the world as a member of an unimportant family, living in a far-off corner of the Roman Empire, speaking a dialect of Greek.

Why not on a white charger with rich clothes, or the son of a Latin-speaking Emperor? Remember that despite the fact that Jesus was born very humbly in a stable, and even though he was very soon a refugee because of Herod, there were those who recognised him – the shepherds, the Magi; and to those who believed was given the gift of life!

And there were people all through his life, and beyond, who were able to recognise him for who he was and is. Even so, there were, and are today, people who are not able to look beyond the rough, outer wrapping to see the promise of what is inside – people with hearts of stone, rather than hearts of flesh.

Prayer

Father God,

at this Christmastide,

we thank you for your gift to us of Jesus.

Help us to recognise him for who he really is,

and to accept him into our lives and show him

to others by what we say and do.

We especially pray for those who are embarrassed

by the name of Jesus, or who take his name in vain.

Pour your love into our world, shine into our lives,

and encourage us to believe.

Amen.

New Year's Revolutions

Aim

To examine our track record when we give ourselves New Year's resolutions, which can be unrealistic. To reflect that one realisable New Year's resolution made to God, rather than many to ourselves, can actually change our lives, and maybe the lives of others – in fact there could indeed be a personal revolution!

Materials

The talk can be given without any aids. But you might consider the following:

- Large picture of a clock showing midnight or an overhead transparency of Big Ben.

- Large poster or overhead transparency bearing the legend, WELCOME . . . *(add appropriate year)*

- Overhead transparency or poster, with the words *NEW YEAR'S REVOLUTIONS*

- Three volunteers from the congregation to act out the parts of Peter, Polly and Min, the children in the poem. Either the children step forward and speak their own lines, or they step forward and the Narrator speaks their lines.

Presentation

Polly's Personal Revolution

Peter, Polly and Min arrived,
at the gate of a brand new year.
And each one willingly contrived,
to bend their father's ear.

With tales of brave new promises,
in boldness they spoke out;
they really thought they'd got it
　　cracked.
Of that there was no doubt.

Their father's head was spinning
　　fast,
with many revolutions,
as each young child reeled off a list
of New Year's Resolutions.

Pete said: 'I'll take the dog for walks,
and answer when Mum calls!
I won't leave dirty fingerprints
on all the bedroom walls.

'I'll do the shopping, wash the car,
whatever is required.
I'll polish windows, vacuum stairs,
even if I'm tired.'

Then Pete sat down and looked
　　around,
a big smile on his face,
as Polly, not to be outdone,
began to speak at pace.

'I'll give up cream and sweets
　　and cakes,
I'll iron all Dad's shirts;
I'll eat up all my vegetables,
and be good until it hurts.

'I'll pull out all the stops at school,
I'll work so hard all day.
I'll get my homework done on time,
and even give up play.

'There won't be any arguments,
I won't be rude to Pete,
I'll be polite to everyone,
I'll be completely sweet.'

It's true the change in Pete and Poll,
would really be surprising;
If they could only keep their word,
they'd be most enterprising.

Poor Minnie paused and drew a
　　breath,
this sounded quite a task.
To match her siblings' bold displays,
was just too much to ask.

So Minnie thought a little while,
and far from coming third,
her plan would put her out in front,
if she could keep her word.

She said: 'I'll not be criticised
for failing to succeed,
rash promises I will not make,
from pressure I'll be freed.

37

She made a pledge to do one thing –
to help to meet the needs
of others maybe seeking help –
a series of good deeds.

A modest little show of care,
to be of some assistance,
to do one small thing every day,
would show the girl's persistence.

You might well guess that when it dawned,
the New Year fresh and bright,
that things were not as easily done,
as the children would have liked.

Pete and Polly found it hard,
in fact, they barely tried,
but word soon spread of Minnie's deeds,
and folk, on her, relied.

So as each day turned to a week,
and weeks all came to pass,
young Minnie made it through the year,
and really showed her class.

The new year soon became the old,
and quickly slipped away.
And Polly did a different deed,
on every single day!

Consolidation

Discuss the merits of the different promises; ask who has actually kept a New Year's resolution. Min succeeded because she made just one promise, which she was able to keep, and it made a difference to so many people's lives. Discuss the kinds of things she might have done to help people, even though she might have had to make sacrifices herself because of this. Can you think of any personal sacrifices Min might have made in order to stick to her promise?

Sometimes God calls people to do things for him. Look at the first disciples. Remember how in that reading from Mark's Gospel (1:16-20), when Jesus called those disciples, they followed him immediately. Their decision meant that they also had to make personal sacrifices . . . but they resolved to follow Jesus. And so they became part of that *REVolution* which was there in Jesus' teaching, preaching and miracles, and of course, which really showed itself with the resurrection.

This new year you might feel that you're being called by God to make a simple kind of resolution like Min, which would make people's lives better.

But sometimes, God calls us to do work for him, which makes even more demands on us than the demands placed on people like Min. When God calls us like this, we can always say 'no'. But so many have said 'yes' . . . and it has made a big difference. Not only to their own lives, but to the world at large, and to the bringing in of the Kingdom of God. And when he does call us like this, even though we might feel afraid, he always provides us with everything we need to do the job.

Prayer

Heavenly Father,

we thank you for this new year . . .

for the challenges and the chances it presents for your people.

Help us to resolve to help people in your name

as much as we can in . . . (*the year just beginning*).

Help us, when you call us to do other special work for you,

to be able to say yes, trusting that you will honour our decision,

and be all we need as we continue our work

to build up your kingdom on earth.

Amen.

In Search of Easter

Summary

Not so much a service, but a suggestion to plan ahead.

Aim

To do some forward planning!

February: This is the time to start thinking about a possible Easter talk. Give away as many daffodil bulbs to your congregation as possible, and provide small plant pots and compost. I know this sounds like one of those daunting talks that begins . . . 'Give every member of your congregation a set of pens and a colouring book . . .' but I have used this talk several times, and it works.

The completed pots then go on the windowsills around church, and someone is given the job of watering them. Lo and behold, by Easter Day, all – or almost all – the daffodils have flowered. New life out of something that seems dead and lifeless.

PS: If you must talk about rabbits at Easter, dress up your curate or other willing helper in a rabbit hire costume, and tell the story of Easter between you, with the aid of an Easter garden that somebody prepared beforehand.

Seriously, it makes a profound impact on the children in particular, and you actually get the chance to tell the story simply. If you wish, use overhead transparencies to help illustrate the talk. Use any resource that helps people to know that Jesus is alive!

Mothering Sunday

Summary   A challenging look at the value we place on mums.

Aim   To remind ourselves not to take our mothers for granted!

A few cautionary notes in case you haven't 'done' Mothering Sunday before:

Remember that although most of us love(d) our mums, there are some whose experience of their mother might not be pleasant. Read the children's novel *Goodnight Mr Tom*, where the young hero, Willie, is traumatised by his mother, and only shown love by Mr Tom. If you feel this is an issue for your congregation, you might read part of this novel aloud if you wish to make a point.

You will most likely have in your congregation women who have never been mothers and women whose children have now left home. Some will be widows, and maybe fairly recently bereaved. At the moment in the service when you invite the children to take small posies to their mothers, ask the children to come back and take a posy and give it to any woman who hasn't yet been handed any flowers, so that every woman takes some flowers away.

Materials
- Overhead transparency or large sign: What is a mother?
- Mum's work grid on overhead transparency or posters, if using Version 1.
- Images for use as overhead transparencies (you could invite a talented artist in the church to produce these before the service, but give them plenty of time).

- Overhead transparencies and actors, if using Version 2.

- Copy of *Ode for Mothering Sunday* if you are using it. (You could invite a twenty-something male to dress up in a school blazer and one of those old-fashioned schoolboy caps, to read the poem. The poem probably doesn't need any explanation!)

- Possibly an extract from *Goodnight, Mr Tom,* by Michelle Magorian. (Published by Puffin Modern Classics, ISBN 0-14-037233-4.)

Talk

Who has ever heard of something called the National Minimum Wage? What is it? How much is it, currently?

How much would our mothers earn a week if they were to be earning the National Minimum Wage for everything they do for us?

Let's have a look at some of the things mums do, and work out how much they ought to be earning a week.

Version 1

Overhead transparency showing what Mum might do for us, and the number of hours she spends doing each task. Here is a specimen. Adapt it to suit local circumstances. It's also worth remembering that sometimes Dad or another helper is also responsible for some of this work!

Work done	Hours spent	Cost (per week)
Cooking		
Cleaning		
Making beds		
Tidying your room		
Ironing		
Washing		
Shopping		
School runs		
Helping with homework		
Taxi service to . . .		
Brownies		
Scouts		
Dancing		
Swimming		
Music lessons . . . etc.		
Total cost		

So often we take our mums for granted. It's only when we see a list like this that we realise how much she does for us, and how much we owe her.

In order to involve some of the elderly members of the congregation, whose mums are probably no longer alive, encourage some of them to tell their own stories about their mums. These stories will probably bring out the fact that many mums in times past sacrificed much for their families. Perhaps try to bring out an amusing incident or two about these mums, in order to lighten things.

Version 2

In this version we are aiming to show not only how much we take our mums for granted when they do so much for us, but also, and perhaps more importantly, how much we take God for granted, when he does so much for us.

A week in the life of Supermum

Picture 1

(Masses of washing up at the sink: Mum up to her armpits; loads of kitchen clutter.)

How many of us recognise this scene? Hands up! There's a saying that cooks should never have to wash up! Look at poor old Supermum! How long will it take her to get the Sunday washing up done?

Fortunately, help is at hand! She has three children who could help her.

She calls them all down into the kitchen.

Picture 2

Same kitchen, same Mum. Three children (Two girls, aged 7 and 15. The 15-year-old's hair is in a towel. Boy, aged about 11, dressed in football kit).

Who's going to help wash up?

John can't. He says he's going out to play football with his mates. Anyway, he washed up on Thursday night. Can't one of the girls do it?

Tracy (teenager): She can't do it, she's just washed her hair. Anyway, she's expecting a phone call any minute from her boyfriend.

Fiona can't. She's just going down the garden to feed Sandy, the rabbit. She suddenly remembered that he hasn't been fed today!

Picture 3

Same kitchen. (Close-up of Mum's face, surrounded by bubbles. Plates, pots, etc., in background.)

No help there, unfortunately. Poor old Mum has to finish the job herself. Let's see what she's doing three days later.

Picture 4

(Reproduce picture 1)

Here she is again. This time, it's Wednesday. And guess what she's doing? Yes, she's washing up again. I wonder if the children are going to help her out tonight?

Picture 5

(Series of speech balloons coming from different corners of the screen saying: Doing my homework! On the phone! Watching Eastenders, etc.).

Picture 6

(Close-up of Mum. She looks angry. She carries a long list of paper which trails on the floor.)

Mum's finished the washing up. It looks as if she's been writing. That's a long list she's holding. Let's have a look and see what's on it. *(Produce a long list and read out the following)*

Dear Children,

I am tired of doing the washing up, the cleaning, the laundry, the shopping, and defleaing the dog all on my own. From now on I'm going to charge the three of you for my services. Here is last week's bill.

Three meals a day for three people	£60
Cleaning bedrooms	£30
Putting away clothes thrown on bedroom floors; emptying waste-paper bins, cleaning the bath, the toilet, the floors and the paintwork	£100
Shopping	£25
Darning, mending and ironing	£30
Answering the telephone to friends	£10
Ferrying to school and back; ferrying to guides, football, dancing, school disco on a Friday night	£50
Laundry bills	£30
Nursing fees: curing headaches, providing hot-water bottles, medicine, cough mixture for people who haven't been feeling very well	£40
Grand total	**£375**

Picture 7

Three children, with tea towels in their hands, sheepishly looking at Mum.

It looks to me as if they want to work off their debt . . . and they seem to be wanting to make a start by doing the washing up!

Consolidation

What was wrong with the children's behaviour?
They took Mum for granted.

How does God feel about it?
How should we treat our mums? The Bible tells us to honour our fathers and mothers.
What does that mean in terms of the way we treat them?

Mums and dads aren't the only ones we take for granted. Many people take God for granted. They make gods out of their possessions, their money or their ambitions. Many people never give God a second thought until they're in trouble. But God wants us to talk to him every day, and never take him for granted. The Bible says: 'You must have no other gods beside me.'

Ode for Mothering Sunday

Oh, I'm *ever* so nice to my mum –
except for the times when I'm not!
I'm usually helpful, consid'rate and kind . . .
a nicer young son to his mum you won't find,
though she has to put up with a lot!

I help her with some of the chores,
and especially with washing the pots . . .
though they tend to stay greasy when washed up by me . . .
I leave smear marks on glasses I just cannot see,
and the tea towel gets tied up in knots.

I've *never* been rude to my mum,
or taken her efforts for granted –
Though I tend to sound off, if she says: 'Make your bed!'
And she'd better be there, when there's pains in my head . . .

But here in my heart, there's planted
a bouquet of roses for Mum . . .
with just one or two thistles as well!
For she sometimes insists that I tidy my room . . .
sweep clean my bad habits with mother's new broom,
or remove my old socks, when they smell!

But my mum is an *angel* to me –
except for the times when she ain't.
For she's got a loud voice – yes, it once shattered glass!
And if she clips your ear, it stays clipped! – let that pass . . .!
No, she isn't a plaster saint.

But today I can say: 'Thank you, Mum!'
For though I can be moody and cross,
you will always forgive, and say: 'Never mind, son . . .'
You know most of the good things and bad things I've done . . .
and I reckon we know who is boss!

(Me on Tuesdays and Fridays . . . Mum, the rest of the week!')

Prayers

Heavenly Father,
we thank you for our mothers,
and for all they have done or are doing for us.
Help us not to take them for granted,
but to honour them according to your will.
In the name of Christ Jesus.
Amen.

Father God,
forgive us when we take for granted
those around us whom we love, and who love us.
And forgive us when we take you for granted,
who love us more than anyone.
In the name of Jesus.
Amen.

Fools Rush In

Summary   Actions and words can happen too quickly – and when they
do there can be regrettable consequences.

Aim   To remember to think before you act and speak: with
special reference to Peter.

Materials

- Banner bearing the words 'Fools rush in where angels
  fear to tread'. (This must be visible from the back, so it's
  best written on the back of a roll of wallpaper and
  gradually unrolled by volunteers from the congregation.)
- A sign saying 'Use your brains'.
- The words 'Think before you act!' on a large sheet of card.
- Two jigsaw puzzles: one on a board, one on a
  tablecloth.
- Balloons.
- Two contestants to prepare for the quiz time in advance.

Presentation

Show the banner bearing the words *'Fools rush in where angels fear to tread'*.

This is a very old saying. It means that we shouldn't do things without thinking about the consequences. It means, use your brains! (Show the sign saying *'Use your brains'*.) Before I carry on I am going to give X and Y a piece of paper each. I'd like them to go over there and make a paper aeroplane while I continue to talk. Here's your sheet of paper and instructions. Make sure you follow them. *(They go off)* Some of my friends have been using their brains, lately. They've been working on a couple of jigsaw puzzles. Here they are with their finished work. *(Two jigsaws are brought in. One is on a board, the other on a tablecloth, and probably falls apart)* As you can see, one group used their brains, and the other didn't.

Board Group	We knew we would be bringing the jigsaw to church today, so we found this nice piece of strong cardboard to carry it on, so it wouldn't fall apart.
Tablecloth Group	We forgot we had to bring our jigsaw to church, so we just started doing it when we got here. We didn't think it through, and when we finished we suddenly realised what we'd done. By then it was too late. We had to bring the jigsaw on a tablecloth.
Narrator	So when we use the expression 'Fools rush in', we are really saying: 'Think before you act'. *(Show the words)*
	Now comes the moment you've all been waiting for. A brand-new quiz show called 'Use your brains!' Here are our two contestants, A and B. They are competing for a prize of £50,000! Now, A and B, we start with a general knowledge round. As soon as you know the answer, hit your opponent on the head with your balloon.
	(Quizmaster gives each a balloon)
Quizmaster	First question. Where is Coronation Street . . .?

(A hits B with balloon, and calls out . . . 'In Manchester')

Quizmaster You didn't hear the full question. B, where is Coronation Street shown? On BBC1, BBC2, ITV, Channel 4 or Channel 5?

B ITV!

Quizmaster Correct! Question 2. What is the first name of the queen . . .?

(A hits B with balloon, and calls out . . . 'Elizabeth')

Quizmaster Wrong! Wait for the full question: B, what is the first name of the queen who ruled England from 1837 till 1901?

B Victoria!

Quizmaster Correct! Last question: Who was JFK?

(A hits B with balloon and says: President of the United States)

Quizmaster Wrong! B, here's the full question: Who was JFK's wife?

B Her name was Jackie Kennedy.

Quizmaster Correct. You win the £50,000!

(Contestants exit)

We'd better have a look at that poster again: *Fools rush in, where angels fear to tread*.

There are examples in the Bible of people who rushed in, without thinking about the consequences. One of them was a friend of Jesus called Simon Peter.

(Jesus enters with some of his friends)

Jesus You have all been my friends for three years. Tomorrow I will die on the cross, but you will all desert me, and you'll be scattered in all directions.

Peter These others might run away and leave you, Master, but I never will. I will always stick up for you and protect you!

Jesus You think so, do you? Let me tell you, Peter . . . even though you speak so boldly, now, by the time the cock crows tomorrow morning at dawn, you will have said three times to people that you never had anything to do with me.

(Jesus and friends go off)

Narrator Soon after that, Jesus was arrested and taken to the house of the Chief Priest to be interrogated. Jesus was right about his friends. Most of them ran away. But Peter hung about in the garden outside the house. He warmed his hands over the fire someone had lit, because it was so cold.

(Enter Peter and two or three others)

Girl *(To Peter)* Make room, please. I want to warm my hands.

Peter Come and stand here. There's plenty of room.

Girl That's a funny accent. You don't come from round here, do you? You sound as if you come from Galilee. Jesus comes from there . . . the one they've arrested. Are you a friend of his?

Peter Never met him before.

Girl I'm sure I've seen you somewhere before. Was it in the temple the other day, with Jesus?

Peter I've never met Jesus. I don't know anything about him.

Girl Yes, I remember, now . . . when Jesus was in the temple. You were with him, together with one or two others.

Peter How many times must I tell you, *I do not know the man*.

(The cock crows)

Peter Oh, Master . . . What have I done . . .?

(He sinks to his knees, and the scene freezes)

Peter was very ashamed, but Jesus was able to forgive him and help him put things right, and he used Peter later on. So remember:

Use your brains. Think before you act. Think before you speak.

Prayer 1

Father God,

help us not to rush in blindly and make promises we can't keep,

or make mistakes because we haven't thought things through.

In the name of Jesus.

Amen.

Prayer 2

Teach us not to be stupid, Lord,

but to use the gift of intelligence

for the benefit of ourselves,

and those around us.

Amen.

Another Point of View

Summary

In large and small ways, we need the help of others.

Aim

To reflect on how we can think of others and make their lives better.

Materials

- Large sheets of card bearing the names of the different people who will speak; or a plain card for those whose character is not given. All the cards carry the script on the back.

- Large box. One side is red with the word 'Danger' written on it; another side is blue with 'Keep Off!' written on it; another green with 'Open Me!' written on it, and the fourth side is black with a white cross on it. The box is covered before the talk starts. Select four volunteers and make them stand where they can see one face of the box.

Presentation

Voice 1 (*Lifting the cover which is hiding the box*) Today I've brought this very special box along. And I'm going to ask each of our volunteers what they can see as they look at the box. (*Elicit answers – some might see two faces of the box: this doesn't matter.*)

From what our volunteers have told us, it's quite clear that they all see something different . . . depending on where they're standing . . . depending on their point of view.

Voice 2 There are many people in the world who have to see things from other people's points of view. For example, a hospital chaplain, a hospice nurse, a prison chaplain, to name but a few.

Voice 3 A hospital chaplain makes time for people who are going through times of stress caused by illness. People might be afraid or worried, or about to have an operation. The chaplain makes time to listen and pray for them. The chaplain is also there to listen to people in hospital or their relatives who are angry because they feel neglected or badly treated.

Voice 4 A hospice nurse has the privilege of caring for seriously ill people and their relatives. She needs a special gift of being able to understand how the people might be feeling. She knows they are still the same as they ever were, despite illness. Friends and neighbours may be too shy and embarrassed to ask how the sick person is, but the hospice nurse can help physically and emotionally.

Voice 5 Industrial chaplains visit offices, shops and factories. They listen to people's problems related to the workplace and help sort out disagreements between bosses and workers. They help working parents find a childminder if necessary; they might spend time with those who are stressed because their business is failing.

Voice 6 Prison chaplains never ask why a person is in prison. Sometimes prisoners want to tell the chaplain and they pour their story out to this person. A prison chaplain can help in practical ways by arranging with the prison governor to escort the prisoner to a dying parent's bedside; by writing letters for those who can't write; by befriending those who are shunned.

Voice 7   We may not do any of these important, caring jobs, but we can think of others and make their lives better.

Voice 8   Here in our church family we can do this. Let me explain how . . .

Voice 9   By meaning it when we ask someone how they are.

Voice 10   By being pleasant to someone we find difficult or don't like.

Voice 11   We can think of the needs of others before our own. When one of our members in church 'go missing' from our congregation, we can make enquiries.

Voice 12   Some of us like to hear the sound of our own voice. We can do less speaking and more listening.

Voice 13   We can avoid mocking those who haven't got the things we have. We can also be thankful for the things we do have, and maybe stop taking them for granted.

Voice 14   We can congratulate people more when they do something clever, or well or good.

Voice 15   We can make the effort to welcome newcomers (even if they occupy the pew we have been sitting in continuously since 1947), and to speak to someone we don't know very well or someone who is on their own.

Voice 16   We can remember that Jesus was never unkind to anyone and never turned anybody away.

Prayer

Father God,

we thank you for one another.

We thank you that we are all different,

and that you treat each one of us as being very special.

Help us to think of the needs and feelings of others,

not only at school or church but in the wider community.

We thank you for all carers, listeners and encouragers,

and we ask you to make us like them.

Amen.

Malteazle *the* Weasel

Summary   God touches all lives.

Aim   To remember that no one is beyond the reach of God, and that God never stops being a God of surprises!

The poem 'Malteazle the Weasel' was inspired by a conversation I once had when I was working in a men's Church of England hostel in the south-west of England. One night, about 2am, I was on duty with the deputy warden. He suddenly said: 'David, did you know that I'm a murderer?'

I did not! – and 2am in a quiet hostel is not the best time to find out!

He told me his story. He had been convicted of murder and sent to prison. There he had come across a prison chaplain who had told him the gospel story simply and yet powerfully. He became a Christian, and entered Christian service.

Materials   In my experience, this needs acting out! Use members of a local primary school for the characters, or members of your junior church. Try to get them to come in costume. There will need to be several rehearsals. Keep movement simple.

Punctuate the various parts by using music from the CD of *Independence Day*, the 1996 science fiction film, together with music from the start of the film *West Side Story*. It is probably best to warn parents of very small children that the action might get boisterous and noisy in places!

Presentation

Keep any preamble to a minimum, so as to optimise the effect of the discovery of Malteazle himself. It is a good idea to have him sitting somewhere prominent during the first part of the service, covered with a blanket. You can keep going to lift the blanket during the service – anything that builds up the anticipation.

Malteazle the Weasel

Malteazle the Weasel had little pink eyes,
and a stare that could freeze up your blood!
A fiend on four legs, he was gone in a flash,
bent on some evil deed – he was reckless and rash,
and was endlessly up to no good!

Now, if they gave prizes for cunning and cheek,
Malteazle would get one tomorrow!
He was King of the Boot Boys on Long Acre Farm,
where the rabbits all swore he was Old Nick's right arm,
for he revelled in trouble and sorrow!

Priscilla the hen got the fright of her life
when Malteazle slunk into her run.
'Get away from my eggs!' she cackled and spat:
'The farmer is coming! – he knows what you're at! –
and he's armed, look: he's got a big gun!'

But no end of guns or of farmers with sticks
could make old Malteazle afraid!
Bring a battering-ram, or a cannon or spear,
you could try to defeat him from now till next year! –
Neither army nor fire brigade . . .

. . . could outwit Big 'M', put a stop to his tricks:
he was feared like a bad dose of measles!
And his infamy spread to the neighbouring farms,
where they shuddered in horror, and set their alarms
against this, the most wicked of weasels!

57

In the dead of the night, this young rascal would meet
with his gang, over which he was chief.
There were ferrets and foxes, a rat with one eye,
a mangy old stoat who had once been a spy;
every one was a villain or thief!

Now his cronies and mates were in fear and in dread
of Malteazle: no heirs or successors
could stand in his way – he would cause their decease!
His methods were shocking, and known to the police,
and studied by long-haired professors!

One day in late August, to Long Acre Farm
came a badger – a preacher of worth.
First he stood on a milk churn and gathered a crowd,
then he spoke about God, in a voice very loud,
and the day Jesus comes back to earth.

Well, the news travelled fast, and he preached for two hours
about sin and salvation to rabbits,
a sty full of pigs, and a duck with no tail –
then against an old goose and two sheep did he rail,
and chastised them for all their bad habits!

When the news of the preacher reached Malteazle's ears
by way of the Bush Telegraph,
he said to his gang: 'Let's get over there, quick,
to where this guy is preaching – we'll give him some stick –
'cos it's months since we've had a good laugh!'

So at his command, they all sprang to their feet
and then into the farmyard they swaggered;
But as Big 'M' took in what the old badger said,
he stopped dead in his tracks. Then he shook his young head,
and his face looked quite weary and haggard.

He spoke not a word till the badger was done.

Then he sank to his knees where he stood!

The gang were embarrassed . . . and crept out of sight . . .

back into the woods under cover of night,

and were very soon up to no good.

For two days, Malteazle he vanished from view,

though according to Horace, the pigeon,

he was spotted alone, wand'ring down by the shore

(A thing which his friends said he'd not done before) –

had he suddenly *Got Religion?*

Well, the very next day, towards late afternoon,

in the farmyard ('til then, quite deserted),

Malteazle appeared – and proceeded to spout

in a very loud voice that fetched all creatures out,

about how he had just been *Converted!*

How different he seemed! – how so suddenly changed!

He had lost all his cunning and viciousness.

He was gentle – and humble – and full of good grace,

of his old wicked self, now, there wasn't a trace,

and he'd lost all his guile and maliciousness.

All the gang were struck dumb by this change in Big 'M',

and they didn't know what to do next;

but they chose a new leader (a thuggish young stoat),

for two pins, they'd have taken Big 'M' by the throat! –

for they certainly were very vexed!

These days, if you ever ask Malteazle why

he's so changed from when he was a lad –

when he used to terrorise Long Acre Farm,

yet is now so approachable, so full of charm –

he will say: 'Well, although I was bad,

'It was all on account of a badger I met

that I've put my wild ways on the rack;

for although he was old – and a little bit odd –

his words touched my heart when he spoke about God,

and what happens when Jesus comes back.'

Prayer

Father God,

we thank you that you want to touch and change the lives of all people.

We thank you for those who have a special ministry of evangelism

and we pray for our own church,

that we will take every opportunity we can

of telling others about Jesus – in whose name we pray.

Amen.

Let's Be the Best of Friends

Summary   It's sometimes easier to lose friends than keep them.

Aim   To think about being loyal to friends; to consider our loyalty
to and friendship for Jesus, and his for us.

Materials   ● Copy of play, *Milo and Dom,* plus props, basic scenery
and costume if desired.

Milo and Dom

(Adapted in play form by the author from a traditional Chinese story)

Narrator Today's play is about being loyal to your friends. Being loyal means you stand by them, you don't do anything behind their back and you always stick up for them. If you stop being loyal to your friends, you'll stop having friends!

This story is about Milo *(enter Milo)* and Dom *(enter Dom)*. Milo and Dom started off being friends – and then something happened!

(Narrator goes off)

Milo It's good to be out in the fresh air, isn't it, Dom?

Dom Yes, especially when the sun's shining like today. Maybe I'll go over there and sunbathe. *(He crosses to the side of the stage)* Hello – what's this? A bag of money!

Milo Are you sure? *(Milo nods his head)* OK then. *(They both go off)*

(Enter a Policeman. Then Milo and Dom re-enter)

Policeman 'Ello, 'ello, 'ello! What 'ave we 'ere then? Aren't you the two boys who brought that bag of money into the police station about three months ago?

Milo That's right, officer. Has it been claimed?

Policeman It has not! Here you are – you're entitled to it, now. Don't spend it all at once!

Dom Thanks, officer! Wow! A thousand silver coins. What are we going to do with it. Let's go home and talk! *(Policeman goes off. Milo and Dom cross down to the corner of the stage)*

Milo Here we are! I suggest we share it between us. We can't tell all our friends about it.

Dom   *(Crosses down to the other corner and speaks to the audience)* But I don't want half of it! I want most of it. I have a wonderful plan! *(He goes back to Milo)* I think we should have just 100 pieces each, and bury the rest under that wall, over there. Then we won't spend it all at once, and we can get some more whenever we need it.

Milo   OK, let's start before anyone sees us. *(They each take a small bag of money out of the larger bag, and cover the rest with some rocks or stones)*

Dom   That's great. Well, it must be tea time, so I'll see you tomorrow. 'Bye.

Milo   See you.

(They both exit)

Narrator   *(Re-entering)* But Dom was very greedy. He soon spent his money, and so he went back to the wall . . . *(Dom re-enters and goes to the wall)* and uncovered the money and ran home with it. *(Dom goes off-stage)* He met Milo again the next day. And he had a question for his friend. *(Narrator exits – Milo and Dom enter from opposite sides of the stage)*

Dom   Hi, Milo! Listen, I need some more money. What about another hundred each? Let's dig the bag up while we're both together, so we'll both know it's fair.

Milo   OK. I want to buy some new clothes with mine. *(He lifts the rocks that were covering the bag)* Oh no! The money bag's vanished. Somebody must have stolen it. But only you knew where the bag was. You must have stolen the money. How could you do that? Pay me back right now – I want half the money.

Dom   I swear I never went near the wall or the bag. I wouldn't steal from you.

Milo   Oh, wouldn't you? I wouldn't put anything past you. You can't be trusted. I was stupid to agree to your plan in the first place.

Dom   Are you calling me a liar?

Milo   Yes – a liar, a thief and a cheat!

(Enter Judge)

Judge   Now, now, now, what's all this noise about? You two have disturbed my afternoon nap. Now I heard what you were both saying – a stolen money bag, eh? A thief and a liar, eh? All very complicated. I'm sure I don't know what to say – and I've been a judge for 30 years!

Dom   The wall! The wall saw what happened – the wall can tell you that I'm telling the truth.

Milo   The wall?

Judge   Walls don't talk – at least, I've never heard one!

Dom   Come back here tomorrow, and I promise you, the wall *will* speak! *(They go off-stage in different directions)*

Narrator   *(Coming back on-stage)* You see – there was another part to Dom's plan that nobody knew about. He told his sister about the money and said she must hide herself behind the wall and pretend to be the wall speaking, and say that it was Milo who stole the money. She wasn't very happy, but she agreed to it . . . so long as she was promised some of the money for herself.

(Exit Narrator. Dom enters, with sister)

Dom   Quickly, now . . . get behind the wall . . . here come Milo and some of his friends. *(Enter Milo, Friends and the Judge)*

Judge   Oh, wall . . .! Tell us who stole the money!

Sister   Milo stole the money!

Milo   That's a lie. I know what's going on! *(He goes behind wall, and drags out Dom's sister)* Here is the voice of the wall – it's Dom's sister.

Sister   Ow! It isn't my fault. I didn't want to do it. Dom forced me!

Judge   Dom, you have been very wicked – very wicked indeed. You must give all the money to Milo. You must even give him your own share. That's your punishment for being such a greedy, disloyal friend.

Dom   That's not fair!

Judge   You were not fair to your best friend, were you?

(Enter Narrator)

Narrator   I don't know whether Milo and Dom stayed friends after that, but I wonder what you would have done, if your friend had been so dishonest and disloyal. Do you think Milo should have forgiven him and stayed friends? I certainly know what I think!

Consolidation

Reflect on the behaviour of the friends in the story, and see how the listeners would answer the narrator's final question. Reflect on the way Jesus' friends treated him, and how he treated them. Jesus was always fair to his friends. Sometimes, this meant he had to say some quite hard things to some of them, but it was always for their own good. One, especially, was Peter. Reflect on Peter's denial.

Prayer

Heavenly Father,

we thank you for our friends.

Help us to value them, and to respect them,

and never treat them dishonestly or be disloyal to them.

In the name of Jesus.

Amen.

The *Person Inside*

Summary   Who are we to judge others?

Aim   To think about the criteria we use in our twenty-first-century world to compare ourselves with one another and consider our own and each others' worth, and to contrast it with the criteria Jesus used to determine someone's value. *Luke 14:1, 7-14.*

Materials
- Six volunteers from the congregation.
- Large cards, each bearing one of the following words: Wealth, Importance, Intelligence, Size, Age.
- Five chairs, with numbers from 1 to 5 on each, with the numbers large enough to be seen from the back of the building.
- Cards with the following professions written on them (again, must be visible from the back): King, Prince, Prime Minister, Tramp, Me.
- Cards: IQ 166; IQ 120; 1Q 111; IQ 110; IQ 86.
- Five cards with £40; £100; £500; £1500; £3500.
- Large card with words 'The person inside' written on it.

Presentation

The Bible reading draws out the fact that so often we compare ourselves with other people. Sometimes we feel we are better, richer, more intelligent or more popular. At other times we feel that we are in other people's shadows, and when this happens we often get jealous.

I've been thinking about how we judge other people, and how we judge ourselves, and I've come up with at least five ways in which we do it. You might think of other ways, but I have five. I'm going to talk about them one at a time.

(I find it best to have each of the words written on a piece of A3 coloured card. Place the cards in order on an easel, for ease of access, but with the backs of the cards showing, so that we can only see what's written on each card when the cards are turned round. Line up the six volunteers in a straight line. The person nearest to you will be Mr Brown, etc. Each time you deal with one of the five ways of judging, a different volunteer becomes 'the judge'.)

WEALTH

Meet Mr Brown. He only judges people by the size of their wallet – by their wealth. *(Hand Mr Brown the Wealth card)* Here are five people he knows. *(Give out cards showing how much everyone earns in a week)* Which of these would Mr Brown think were most worth knowing? Yes, the one who earns £3500 a week. *(Place that person on chair 1)* This person gets the most important place. *(Put the rest of the people in rank order, according to how much they earn. Get the congregation to help you decide what the order should be.)*

What are the dangers of judging ourselves and others according to how much money we earn?

(Elicit answers from the congregation.)

I've just been reading a story called *The Little Princess,* where a girl called Sara goes to a new school. She is very rich, and everybody treats her like a princess. But her father loses all his money, and the people she lives with turn her into a servant, take all her fine things away, and make her sleep in the attic with the rats and mice.

When they find out at the end of the story that her father's money hadn't been lost at all, but she is richer than she ever was, they want to be friends with her again – but you can imagine how she feels. She isn't nasty to them, but she knows why they are trying to be friends, and she won't have anything to do with it.

IMPORTANCE

Meet Miss White. She judges people purely on their importance – their position in society. *(Hand out the profession cards, and work out with congregation who should be in chair 1 and what the rest of the rank order might look like, according to the criterion of importance.)*

What are the dangers of using IMPORTANCE and POSITION in society for our method of judging others and ourselves? There's a true story about a student at Trinity Theological College, where vicars are trained, who dressed as a tramp and sat for a whole morning at the gate of the college. The events of the morning were recorded on video, and it was surprising how many Christian students studiously avoided or ignored the person!

INTELLIGENCE

Here's Mrs Jones. She judges people purely on their intelligence. *(Hand out IQ cards, and work out with congregation who should be in chair 1 and what the rest of the rank order might look like, according to the criterion of intelligence.)*

SIZE

Mr Smith judges people on how tall they are. The taller the better, as far as he is concerned! *(Put the group of volunteers into rank order, according to height)* When we judge simply by what a person looks like – their height, size, weight, looks, and so on – we miss other things, like the kind of person they really are or how they get on with other people.

AGE

Mrs Green, here, always judges people according to their age. She believes small children should be seen and not heard, and that old people are only fit for the scrap heap. Some people use this a lot to judge people and decide how worthwhile or valuable they are. Many older people don't have a good word to say about the young, and many young people call older people wrinklies and think they are past it. But there was a clergyman who, while still a very young 80-year-old, used to go into a residential care home every

Christmas to give the 'old' people their Christmas dinner. Most of the people concerned were in their 60s and 70s!

Consolidation

Well, we could go on. But I want to finish by looking at that passage from the Bible again, asking this question. How did Jesus judge people when he was deciding who would be first and who would be last? He didn't use any of the methods we've been thinking about today. He simply looked at what most of us cannot see. The person inside. *(Show final A3 card with 'The person inside' written on it)* He could tell what a person was like inside – and whether they were Jesus' friend and were ready to follow him and do the things he wanted them to do for God's sake. He asks us questions:

- Do you love me?

- Do you trust me?

- Do you put me first?

- Do you show me to others?

- Does my light shine through you?

If we can answer 'yes,' then we are sure of a high place in the kingdom of Heaven. Those whose person inside was looking at Jesus and showing Jesus to others are the ones who will be in the seats of honour in Jesus' kingdom.

But what if we have answered 'no' to some or all of those questions? Don't despair – Jesus still cares for us and wants to do his part to make us perfect.

The story we heard read from the Bible reminds us that there is plenty we have to do to make our own person inside perfect, but that Jesus gives us plenty of help.

On my computer I have a program called Cleansweep. It clears away all the junk and rubbish I have collected in my computer. All I have to do is push a button and it does its job. We all need something called Cleansweep in our lives, to make the person inside the one Jesus wants us to be. Jesus himself provides the Cleansweep we need. This helper is called the Holy Spirit. He alone can get rid of all the rubbish in our hearts and minds. As far as he is concerned, we can't push a button to make him work. But we can pray and ask him to work. And the wonderful thing is – he always does.

Prayer

Heavenly Father,

forgive us when we judge ourselves to be better than others,

and take for ourselves the place of honour when it is reserved

for somebody who deserves it much more than we do.

Help us to be humble as we think about the worth of other people,

remembering that everyone is valuable to you.

Help us to give the person inside each of us to you,

so that you can make us fit to receive Jesus,

to tell others about him,

and to do your work in your twenty-first-century world.

Amen.

Perkin
and the
Ants

Summary   An inspiration to get stuck in.

Aim   To show that churches are not one-man bands, but that members need to work together for the building of God's kingdom, and that selflessness, not selfishness, is needed for this to happen.

Materials
- Copy of poem, 'Perkin and the Ants'.
- Overhead transparencies: pictures to accompany poem.

Presentation

I have an ants' nest just outside my back door. It's been there for more than five years. Every year I do my very best to destroy it. I must have tried everything by now, but still the ants keep coming back. What do you think is the secret of their success?

(Hopefully the answer will emerge that the ants all work together for the common good. There is no such thing as selfishness in a colony of ants.)

A church, if it's doing its job properly, will be like a colony of ants. Here's a poem, which perhaps explains why.

Perkin and the Ants

O, what are you staring at, Perkin the Cat,
as you sit with your wide, green eyes
so stonily fixed on a part of the path
that leads from the flower bed to the bird bath?
What takes you so much by surprise?

'I'm staring at dozens of little black ants
who have made a nest under this bush.
They're all working at more than 100 per cent!
What a furious pace – and how firm their intent,
as around and about they all rush.

'See – they all pull together! I can't understand
why they bother! That wouldn't suit me!
For cats hunt alone, and all company shun!
In working for others, I can't see the fun!
I'm a cat! And cats have to be free!'

Oh, why do you work so hard, little black ants?
You have quite confused Perkin the Cat.
For cats please themselves – as this one's just confessed;
yet you work as a team, for the good of the rest.
Now, not even people do that!

73

At this, one ant spoke up – he stood close by the nest,
watching colleagues arrive and depart.
'What a lot you cats miss!' said the ant with a squeak.
'We all work together – the strong and the weak –
like a body, that's got many parts.

'We're a team, we're a band, we're an army of might!'
continued the ant, quite entranced.
'Whereas you live a life where you don't care for any,
we work as a brotherhood – slave for the many –
now, don't you think that's quite advanced?'

'But only the fittest survive in this world!'
sulked the cat. 'And above everything,
a mean reputation is what I prize most!
I'll knock all other felines from pillar to post,
for of all cats, I want to be king!

'I am simply the greatest, most cunning, most sly,
most incredibly brave in the fight!
I have scrapped with the bravest at mid-afternoon,
oh yes, I've been the piper, and I've called the tune,
and I've danced a mad war dance at night!

'I'm for me, not for him or for you or for them,
but for me!' and his back arched with pride.
Then his fine whiskers twitched as he purred at the thought.
'No, that won't do at all! That's not what ants are taught!'
said the ant – and he scurried inside.

Well, he shook himself off as he entered the nest,
and thought: 'Humble? that's what Perkin ain't!'
Told his brothers and sisters – and everyone laughed
at the cat's wild ideas. 'How deliciously daft!'
they guffawed, 'How incredibly quaint!'

Well, it's long ago, now, since young Perkin gave vent

to his views about black ants' affairs;

for just over two weeks, he was king of all cats

in the district: was feared by the dogs and the rats –

oh my goodness, he put on such airs!

Then quite suddenly, one afternoon before tea,

he fell out with one of his wives.

His continual boasting annoyed this poor puss,

who on seizing her chance, pushed him under a bus! –

where he lost all nine of his lives!

It was goodbye to Perkin! The ants were quite sad:

there was no one to shed any tears.

'And the ants? Do they still work as one?' you might ask.

Yes – they've all pulled together – still bent on their task

for just about 2000 years.

Consolidation

Talk with the congregation generally about the differences between the ants and Perkin. How easy it is to become arrogant and proud when we think we are our own boss. Remember the wife? Why did she get so angry? Do we know people like Perkin? *(Without, of course, mentioning any names!)*

Talk about the fact that the early Church took very seriously the idea of working together. The scriptures tell us about how they shared things with one another, and truly worked as the Body of Christ – and the scriptures also tell us of how things sometimes went wrong in the early Church because of people's selfishness or self-importance, or desire to go their own way. What lessons does all of this have for the Church in our own day?

Let's finish by thinking of one thing our church could do, so that we can work more closely together.

Prayer

Father God, we thank you that we are members of your Church.

Help us to work together in friendship, and to use our gifts in your service.

In the name of Jesus,

Amen.

Touch

Aim

To show how this God-given sense should not be taken for granted, and to show how it can be used for our good.

Materials

- Large cards bearing the name of each of the five senses.
- Five 'feely bags' (plastic bags with objects placed inside them).
- Tactile baby books (books with pictures of animals, etc., which are made of different kinds of material so that each feels different).
- Copy of the story. Present it on a piece of folded A3 card, with a picture or writing on the front, so that it looks as if you have taken trouble over it. A large picture of an ant, perhaps, carrying a blind person's white stick.

Presentation

Volunteers hold up a card bearing names of five senses. Say that you are going to focus on touch today.

We know that babies can hear things when they are still inside their mums; and can see things, even though they are a bit blurry, from the moment they are born. But they can also enjoy touching things from a very early age. Take this feely book for example. Babies love looking at the pictures and feeling the different textures of the animals in it. How many of you have ever had a feely book?

I like running my hand through water when I'm being taken for a ride in a rowing boat or touching newly mown grass or a bright new spring leaf. What sort of things do you like the feel of?

God has given us the gift of touch, but we can use it well or badly. How would you feel about a person stroking a little puppy? How would you feel about someone spanking a little puppy? (Elicit some answers.)

Touch is a very important sense. Here are five plastic bags. We can't see what's inside them. But I'm going to ask each of my volunteers to feel the bags and see, just by touching the contents, if they know what's inside. (Beforehand fill the bags with fairly obvious things: banana, doll, book, plate, cup, can of food, etc.)

It is obvious that even though we can't see, we can use the gift of touch.

We said earlier that touch can be used in good and bad ways. Here's a little story – see if you think it tells us anything about this.

Anthony, the Brave Little Ant

I'm going to tell you a story about someone called Anthony. Anthony was an ant, and he lived with hundreds of his brothers and sisters in the ants' nest down at the bottom of Mr and Mrs Brown's garden.

Anthony was different from his brothers and sisters. He was blind. He had been blind ever since he had been born. He couldn't see a thing.

Well, I'm sorry to say that Anthony's brothers and sisters were very unkind to him because of this. They poked him, pushed him, tapped him on the shoulder and on the head and turned him round and round and made fun of him. He couldn't defend himself because he couldn't see who was doing it, or where they were.

He got so cross and upset that in the end, he decided to go and see his mother, who was the queen of the ants. Her name was Matilda. Queen Matilda lived in a very special room right in the middle of the ants' nest. She was guarded by a bunch of very fierce-looking soldier ants, and she was so important that Anthony had to book an appointment with her two whole days in advance.

His mother, the Queen, was quite sympathetic, but she didn't really know what she could do to help him. She did decide to round up a few of the younger ants who had been causing trouble in other parts of the nest, but they promised the Queen they had done nothing wrong, and had never been anywhere near Anthony, and were sure they wished him well. They said that nobody had touched, shoved or pushed him, and that he must have dreamed it.

The Queen seemed satisfied, but she did send them all to bed without their supper, just to be on the safe side, and then the matter was closed.

That night in bed, the naughty ants all got together to decide how to punish Anthony for getting them into trouble, when suddenly there was a strange smell. It was the smell of smoke. Moment by moment, the whole nest was being filled with a horrible smoke that stopped the ants from seeing where they were going and made them choke and cough. It was actually the work of Mr Brown. He had decided that the ants had been in his garden long enough, and he had lit a fire over the top of the nest. The poor ants. What could they do? They couldn't see a thing. They would never find their way to safety. They would all be killed.

Suddenly the poor ants heard a voice they recognised.

'It's me – Anthony!' said the voice. 'I can lead you all to safety. I don't need eyes to find my way out of this nest. I've done without eyes all my life. One of you touch me on my shoulder, and hold on. The rest of you hold on to each other so we form a long, joined-up line. I'll take you all to safety.'

The poor ants had no choice. The eldest one – the one who had done most to hurt Anthony – touched him on his shoulder, and clung on for dear life. All the rest joined in a long line, and very, very slowly, using his stick to touch the side of the walls, Anthony led them all to safety – even the Queen, who was carried to safety by some of her soldiers.

Out in the fresh air, the ants were raving about Anthony and how he'd saved them. The ones who had hurt him apologised and said they would never do it again! The Queen thanked him personally, and then the task began of finding a new place for a brand-new nest. As for Anthony, everybody loved him from that moment – and you can be sure that he was never teased or tormented again.

Talk about the way in which touch is used negatively and positively in the story. You can also develop the idea of bullying – especially those apparently weaker than us, or those who are somehow different.

The Bible tells us how Jesus used the sense of touch, usually to heal people. Once there was a man who was blind. Jesus touched his eyes, and he could see again. Sometimes, people touched Jesus and they were made better. There was a lady who had been poorly for several years, who knew that if she just touched the hem of Jesus' robe, she would be healed. And so she was.

Prayer

Father God,
we thank you for all our senses,
but particularly today for our sense of touch.
May we never take this special sense for granted.
Help us to recognise that it can be used for good and bad things,
and help us always to use it for good.
Amen.

Dehydrated: *after a* Fashion . . .

Aim   To remind us that we need to *listen* to each other and not to be so wrapped up in our own preoccupations that we ignore one another or one another's needs. To remember that each one of us is special. Also, to remind us to listen to God, and not to take him for granted.

Presentation

(The Headmaster is discovered, reading a newspaper. Enter Jones with a pile of marking.)

Jones   Morning, Headmaster.

Head   Morning, Smith.

Jones   Jones.

Head   What? How's your wife, these days? Rosemary, isn't it?

Jones   Rachel. She's not been well, I'm afraid.

Head   *(Without looking up from his newspaper)* Oh, good . . . good . . . What about those three girls of yours?

Jones   They're boys . . . and there are only two of them.

Head   Hmmm? Quite right . . . boys, of course!

(Pause)

Jones   Can I talk to you privately for a moment, Headmaster?

Head   Hmmm? Fourteen down . . . 'Dehydrated: after a fashion . . .'

Jones   Do you mind, Headmaster? Only, I've got to talk to someone!

Head   'Someone . . .' No, it's only four letters. 'Dehydrated: after a fashion . . .'

Jones   It's this job, you see. I don't really think I'm cut out to be a teacher, after all. My class are rude and noisy, and they never shut up. I'm weeks behind with my marking, and the people who have to teach next to my room are always complaining about how I can't control my classes or shut them up. I thought I liked Physics, but that was before I had to try and teach it! You try teaching Physics to 28 children who just don't want to know!

Head   'Dehydrated: after a fashion'. No . . . blessed if I can get it. Oh, sorry Smith . . .

Jones   Jones!

Head   Yes, yes . . . quite so. Now what was it you were saying? Something about Physics, wasn't it? Well, you know, you'd be much better asking your Head of Department . . . Mrs Jones . . .

Jones   Smith!

Head   Ah, yes! You'd be much better talking to her if it's a question of Physics. Not my subject, you see. I'm a History man, myself.

Jones   Well, I've tried talking to Mrs Smith about my problems, Headmaster, but she's always so busy . . . you know . . . never really has time . . .

Head   Yes . . . nearly ten o'clock. The bell for next lesson will be going in a minute.

Jones   No, she never has time enough to spare. Always having to rush from one lesson to the next. Then there's the sport I've been asked to do. I know when I came for my interview I said I'd be glad to coach a cricket team. I've done quite a bit in that line, as I expect you know. But at the beginning of this term, the Deputy Head asked me if I'd run the under-15 soccer team, and help with cross-country. And when the Head of Music found out I could play the trumpet, she roped me into the orchestra. I've only been in the school three terms, and already I feel busier than an air-traffic control officer at Heathrow Airport.

Head   Heathrow Airport? Heathrow Airport? Terrible place. Lost the mother-in-law for seven whole hours there, last summer. They said it was a mix-up with the passports. Terrible do, the whole thing. Ten more minutes, and she would have been on her way to Zanzibar!

Jones   . . . Anyway, my wife said I ought to talk to you about it. Have a good heart-to-heart . . . you know . . . put all my cards on the table. 'He's sure to understand . . .' she said. 'You go along and have a little chat with him.'

Head   You know, you and your wife, Rosemary . . .

Jones   Rachel!

Head   What?

Jones   My wife . . . she's called Rachel!

Head   Yes, well anyway, you and your wife and daughters really must come and have lunch with us, before too long. Give us a chance to get to know you a little better.

Jones   But listen . . . you don't seem to understand! Don't you see that I'm nearly going up the wall?

Head   Good . . . Good! That's settled then. I'll get my wife to give Rosemary a ring. Oh, by the way, since you're here, I wanted to ask you a small favour. We're short of someone to take the Year 11 mixed hockey team – and I think we're rather counting on you!

PS. In case you tried to solve the crossword clue – it was simply a red herring.

Consolidation

Discuss the lack of communication going on in the sketch. The playlet reminds us how easy it is not to hear what people are saying – not to be interested in them – not to notice when they are in real need – to be too preoccupied to notice or care. Jesus was often surrounded by people in real need. He never turned anybody away. He was profoundly interested in people – not necessarily for who they were or for what other people thought about them, but for themselves. Often the religious leaders were surprised when they found out the kinds of people Jesus was mixing with. *(Give examples: Zacchaeus, woman taken in adultery, etc.)* But Jesus was interested in these people, and particularly in helping them to be whole.

Jesus is interested in you and in me. Nothing is more important to him, in fact, than our welfare. He knows everything there is to know about us – we can't hide anything from him. There is a lovely old hymn that we sometimes have at Holy Communion. In it we have the chance to tell Jesus that we come to him, whatever our doubts, our failings and our needs. *(Read out any part of 'Just as I Am' which you think particularly fits your congregation.)* People often love this hymn, because it is so real. There are other hymns and choruses that perhaps make too many claims for some people. There is one that has the words, 'Here I am, wholly available . . .' Jesus often met with, and indeed helped and healed, people who were not wholly available. It is his wish that we should become wholly available – but he often has to do a work of healing in us before we reach that blessed state.

Part of the message today is that we need to *listen* to each other and get to know one another really well. Maybe there is someone at school, in the office or the shop where you work, or even at home who you have known for years – and yet have not really known. Maybe now is the time to do something about it. And as you do that, you can be sure that if you listen to God, and don't take him for granted, he will show you in no uncertain terms how interested he is in you, and what wonderful things he has planned for your life. At home, we have a plaque hanging on a wall. It says 'Prayer changes things'. Listen to God – talk to him – and you will see for yourself just how true that is, and just how interested in you he is.

This talk could obviously go in several different directions. Do what you feel prompted to, after reading the sketch. But do prepare what you are going to say beforehand!

Prayer

Just as I am, though tossed about
with many a conflict, many a doubt,
fightings within, and fears without,
O Lamb of God, I come.
Amen.

Charlotte Elliott (1789–1871)

Extension materials

If you wish to work on the subject of the specialness and uniqueness of individuals, and are working with children, you might find this poem of use.

You, me and us

I hope you can see
that there's only one me,
and I'm not a bit like you.
I've two eyes and a nose,
two ears, I suppose,
and teeth that love to chew . . .
But we're diff'rent, you see,
her . . . him . . . you . . . and me . . .
and each with our own point of view.

We're not quite the same,
now, no one's to blame:
that's how it was meant to be . . .
the things that we think,
the way that we blink . . .
we're different, can't you see?
I'm tall . . . you're short . . .
mine is music, yours, sport,
you like coffee, but I like tea.

I'm unique,
the way I speak
is not the same as you:

85

I have my say
in my own special way,
we've differing points of view.
And if you don't know,
it was God made it so:
believe it: 'cos it's true!

Don't Keep It Under Your Hat

Aim

To remember that church isn't a Sunday club, but that we are told by Jesus to take the gospel out into the world.

Materials

- Top hat or similar as a handy prop.
- The name 'Jesus' and the phrase 'The Good News!' written on fluorescent card, easily seen from the back.
- A rubber spider, obtained from a joke shop or theatrical suppliers.
- A copy of the poem, pasted onto a card that has upon it the picture of a large spider. It may be useful to have different people reading different parts of the poem, planted in different places, to give it variety.
- Overhead transparencies to illustrate the poem.
- The words 'Perseverence' and 'Ambition' written large on card.

Presentation

Show spider – do you like spiders?

(Engage with the congregation about who does and does not like spiders, and the reasons why.)

Here's a riddle for you – see if you can work it out. Why is a spider like St Paul? Because they are both very determined. And they both had great ambition! Do you have any ambitions? What are they?

(Ask the same question of the adults, and particularly focus on any unrealised ambitions, and the reasons why they remained unrealised.)

Last week, I saw a wonderful spider's web on one of my rose bushes. It must have taken hours to make, and it was absolutely perfect. But then somebody destroyed the web, and when I came back an hour later, it was gone. But the spider was still there. And the next day, there was a new web, all spick and span, and there was Mr Spider, sitting stock still in the middle of it. That spider wasn't going to be stopped! St Paul was a bit the same. He knew he had a mission, and he wasn't going to be stopped. Even if that meant that he had to go to prison for what he believed. And he did spend lots of time in prison in Rome, and 40 days in Philippi in Greece – and all because he couldn't stop doing what he knew he was born to do.

Do you know what Paul was born to do? It wasn't to make spiders' webs. It was to tell other people about the Good News of Jesus.

A friend of mine – a vicar – was once asked why we need to bother telling other people about the Good News of Jesus – especially people in foreign countries. After all, there are enough people in England needing to hear the Good News, never mind people abroad. But my friend answered by recalling what Jesus said at the end of Matthew's Gospel. Let me read it to you.

> Therefore go and make disciples of all nations, baptising them in the name of the Father and of the Son and of the Holy Spirit, and teaching them to obey everything I have commanded you. And surely I am with you always, to the very end of the age. (Matthew 28:19, 20)

The following little poem I found is all about a spider. He would never give in . . . just like Paul.

Happiness . . . Is Web-shaped!

At a quarter past eight by the clock in the hall
(it was August, not April or Feb),
a spider the size of a 20-pence coin
clambered up through a knot-hole, where two floorboards join,
and declared: 'I shall spin me a web!'

As the clock struck the half he was well up the stairs,
but eyes fixed on a spot on the banister.
Soon, he'd spun a few yarns where the staircase turns right;
then a youth dashed upstairs – giving spider a fright –
as he drank from a large Pepsi canister!

'What's all this?' burped the youth, and he gave a loud sniff
as he spied on the spider's *chef d'oeuvre.*
With a flick of the can, spider's yarns were dispatched –
eight long legs scuttered sideways – a door was unlatched –
and a voice cried: 'Is that you, our Merv?'

Well, as Merv left the scene, spider blinked both his eyes,
then surveyed the electricity meter
tucked under the stairs. But the spot was too dark
to entrap many flies – so he thought he would park
on a photo of Merv's sister, Rita . . .

that was stood on a table just under the clock,
and was framed with two ivory tusks . . .
And he'd spun half a web there, by just after ten,
when a toddler skipped out of the kitchen, and then
demolished the web, with two rusks!

Well, it made spider spin (if you'll pardon the pun!),
then he sighed and said: 'Nil desperandum!
I shall not be defeated! – for something within
keeps prodding me on, saying: 'Spin, spider, spin
a new web!' Just choose somewhere at random!'

Between ten and eleven he tried three times more
to spin him a web: and though deft
at his craft, he was thwarted at every attempt.
Each time something happened: no web was exempt,
till he couldn't tell warp from weft!

He was reeling a bit when it got time for lunch,
so he rested awhile – in a cavity
just under the windowsill in the front room
then he sighed just a little bit, there in the gloom,
and adjusted his centre of gravity.

But he grew more determined around two o'clock,
to spin webs that were gossamer thin.
He announced to the world (and his little eyes popped):
'I was born to make cobwebs! I shall not be stopped!
Let them try it! They never can win.'

He was true to his word. For by twenty past five,
he'd fulfilled his frustrated vocation,
and the best web that spider had ever created
hung over the kitchen door – gently vibrated –
And lured all the flies in the nation.

Oh, spider was glad that he'd not been put off
when he saw how the web caught the flies.
And he knew he'd been right, and had seen the thing through –
for a spider must do what a spider must do
from his birth, till the moment he dies!

Consolidation

If the spider had anything, he had perseverance *(have this word written on a card)*. Tease out what this means to the spider, and apply it to our own lives. Jesus had great perseverance – many people tried to stop him doing his work among the people while he was a grown-up in Palestine, but the more they tried to stop him, the more he defeated them. The spider in the story not only had perseverance, but also ambition *(show on card)*. Jesus had great ambition – not for himself, but for the world. His ambition was for everybody in the world to come to the Father through him. And his ambition for those who believe and trust in him today is that they will tell other people about him, so that they might stand a chance of coming to the Father through him. The spider was trying to build something – a web. Jesus is trying to build something – his Church. It's made up of lots of people – all different, but all joined together because of their love for him. It is our job to help him to build, and to fulfil his great ambition for the people of the world.

Prayer

Father God,

we thank you for the fact that Jesus

never gave up his great ambition for the world.

We thank you that we can help him build his church

and tell people about him in our own way.

Help us to believe and trust in him,

and to share what we know of him with others.

Amen.

How Does Your Garden Grow?

Aim

To remember that as members of the church we can either prevent growth or encourage it.

This talk can easily link in with the story of *Perkin and the Ants,* from an earlier service.

Materials

- OHT of a one-man band, showing how frustratingly impossible it is to play all the instruments at once. *(You could invite a person to produce this drawing for you – it will also help you to make the point concerning use of gifts. But make sure you give the person enough time to work on the drawing.)*

- Copy of *The Ballad of the Three Gnomes* and, if you think it's desirable, overhead transparencies illustrating the poem.

Presentation

Invite the congregation to recall times they've been let down by people – a delivery man who promised to come on Tuesday but didn't arrive till Saturday; the man who said he'd prune your apple tree and made a complete mess of it; the person who said: 'Don't you worry – just leave it to me!' and two months later you're still waiting for them to do the job.

There are sometimes people at work, school or church who promise to do things, or whom we ask to do things, but who let us down. It often makes us want to do the jobs ourselves, knowing that at least they will be done properly. We often think we can make a better job of something than the next person. When this sort of attitude exists in a church, we are in danger of excluding people and their gifts. And sometimes there are people at school, at work or in church who want other people to do all the work. There's very little room in this world for passengers. When people refuse to help, the person in charge doesn't have much choice but to do the work him or herself. Nothing is more crippling than a one-man band. Take a look at this picture of one.

There are some people who, although it's hard, do allow others to use their gifts and talents, whether at school, at work or in church. When we do this, we often find ourselves left with the jobs that we don't much like doing. George Carey, who used to be the Archbishop of Canterbury, told a story of how he was working in a church in the north of England and wanted to try to get everyone working together and using their talents. They did this, but he found himself left with the job of printing out the magazine, because other people were doing all the other exciting jobs. But he didn't mind, and we know that God blessed that church and its work.

Here is a poem about three gnomes. One of them gives other people jobs to do and they let him down. Another one wants to do everything himself, with disastrous results and the third one – well, I'll leave you to decide what happened to him!

The Ballad of the Three Gnomes

One Monday night, if you'd been walking
down Great Windsor Street,
and passed by all the gardens there,
you might have heard upon the air
the tramp of marching feet!

For on the second Monday
past the 28th of May,
the garden gnomes from round about,
they meet together – all get out
and have a holiday.

For gnomes, you see, spend all the year
a-managing their gardens;
yes, they're in charge, and what is more,
to garden folk their word is law
(begging their owners' pardons!).

And when a gnome knows all his stuff,
just watch his garden flourish!
Everything happens as he's planned:
the garden folk eat from his hand,
he'll tend and care and nourish

all things within his own domain
(they say that's how God planned it).
But, oh! – there came, that Monday night,
three gnomes caught up in conclave tight,
who couldn't understand it!

Grandfather gnome, a nice old chap,
put down his walking stick –
told how his garden grew with weeds,
how slugs had eaten all his seeds –
poor Grandpa felt quite sick!

He'd asked the worms to dig a trench
to put some seedlings in.
They'd all refused the task, and said:
'We've better things to do, instead!'
Excuses tired and thin . . .

he got from ladybirds, when asked
to chase some greenfly off.
The bees, when pressed to do some work,
just buzzed a bit, and gave a smirk,
and then began to scoff.

The starlings laughed, when he asked them
to clear the lawn of litter.
The sparrows flew away instead,
when asked to weed the flower bed –
you should have heard them twitter!

And so the old gnome's garden was
distinctly overgrown.
Too old himself to do the tasks,
he's given up: now never asks
for help, but sits alone

and ponders on what might have been
had everyone been doing
everything that they'd been told.
'But it's no use – I'm far to old –
Let it go to rack and ruin!'

And all the creatures living there,
since it was such a mess,
they simply went off on their own
to pastures new: the birds have flown
and left this wilderness.

The second gnome, a pleasant chap,
who wore a cap and bell,
said: 'Garden folk? They just can't work!
Even the simplest task they shirk!'
He wasn't feeling well!

'They never do things properly,
but leave the jobs half done.
Their work's distinctly second-rate!
I want the *best* (a word they hate!) –
they like things to be fun.

'But no one ran a garden yet,
where things were second best.
I gave up asking long ago
if they'd all help – they're much too slow,
when they're put to the test.

'And it's no joke, believe you me,
being this one-man band.
I'm working day and night, don't stop –
press on until I'm fit to drop,
with never a helping hand.

'There's not much progress, you can bet –
and me? I'm feeling ill!
It's crippling, working at this pace,
as day by day, my tail I chase,
run fast – just to stand still!'

The third gnome didn't speak at first,
when silence reigned at last.
He just stood still – and blinked his eyes
at both his friends, in mild surprise,
and then looked on, aghast.

'I'm very worried, friends,' he said
at last, in consternation.
'Because my garden's not like yours:
I use – to get help with the chores –
the art of delegation.

'My garden folk all have their place:
each midge, frog, wasp in turn –
they're an accommodating lot,
so grateful for the things they've got –
there's much you have to learn!

'My garden runs like clockwork, friends,
now don't look quite so peeved!
And everything so smoothly runs –
it just ticks on – it purrs and hums,
and so much is achieved.'

Well, 12 months passed, until again
the gnomes took holiday.
But two small gnomes did not appear,
to join that threesome of last year –
they'd vanished, clean away!

For old gnome's garden grew so wild,
its owner dug it up!
Put paving slabs where once were shrubs –
banished the ladybirds and grubs!
Bitter the old gnome's cup!

He ended soon his garden days –
they took him on a trip,
along with all the garden trash
they couldn't sell to friends for cash,
and dumped him on the tip!

As for the young gnome who would not
give garden folk their head,
he worked his fingers to the bone,
was found one day, all on his own,
upon the lawn: quite dead!

The one gnome left, he sighed and said,

'I cannot fathom those

who missed their opportunity!

How sad they now will never see

how fair the garden grows!'

Don't Just
Sit There...
Do Something!

Summary

Spreading the news.

Aim

To remind ourselves that evangelism won't happen by itself . . . we need to do our bit!

Materials

- Copy of *Willie the Worm*.

- Possibility of materials from a missionary organisation such as Wycliffe Bible Translators, explaining a little about their work. Most organisations now have websites and it is straightforward to pull things from there and turn them into handouts or overhead transparencies.

- If possible, a worm puppet or toy (available from toyshops). I have used a slightly doctored caterpillar!

Presentation

(a) If using a puppet. Talk to the puppet and get the children to ask him questions. He could ask the children (or adults) questions. Ask him where he lives *(Down at the bottom of the garden)* and if he does any work *(No, just sits around all day: but he IS famous! There is a poem written about him)*. Read the poem aloud, maybe using overhead transparencies.

(b) If not using a puppet. Talk about your cousin Herbert, who spends most of his life in bed. He doesn't have a job, and is not particularly well-motivated to do anything – he enjoys being lazy. Ask why that is dangerous. Here's a poem about 'Willie the Worm' – he was lazy, too.

Willie the Worm

Now one day in the garden, a little brown worm –
name of Willie – was having a snooze.
Right under a stone he had wriggled, and slept,
for he hadn't a moment to lose:

'Cos he'd worked very hard all the morning, at digging
a tunnel beneath the rose bed.
So when afternoon came, he was tired, and he dozed,
till a voice just behind him said:

'Are you Willie the Worm? – well, I want to be friends.
Oh, I'm sorry! did I wake you up?
My name is John Christopher. How do you do?
Why not come 'ome with me and let's sup?'

'But I know nowt about you!' said Willie, quite shocked,
and he wriggled his tail in surprise.
'You must never trust strangers! Now all worms know that!'
But at once in John Christopher's eyes

young Willie the Worm saw a flicker of warmth
that instantly put him at ease.
So he happily went to John Christopher's place,
and ate haddock and soft mushy peas.

Now as the days passed, little Willie made friends
with JC – he became his best mate.
And they never fell out, nor had a cross word . . .
They were pals, I'm so glad to relate.

'Now listen 'ere Willie,' said JC one day,
'there's a job that I'd like you to do.
For it's come to my notice there's other young worms
in the garden, and I've chosen you

'to introduce me to your pals in the yard.
Do say that you'll help, double quick!
For I want to make friends with 'em all, and learn more
about what makes you little worms tick!'

Young Willie went silent a minute or two –
then he begged John Christopher's pardon
and said, yes, he'd help to make his best friend known
to the rest of the worms in the garden.

'I knew I could count on you, Will,' said JC.
'Now jump to it, young feller-me-lad!'
So off Willie went. Oh, but he dragged his tail –
and inside – well, he felt pretty bad!

He didn't like sharing his new friend, you see,
with the whole population of Wormery.
He was jealous, I guess, and his stomach felt sick,
till he wished he was in the Infirmary.

There were dozens of worms in the garden that day,
with John Christopher dying to meet them.
But Willie grew stubborn, and dug in his heels!
And gave JC no chance to greet them.

'Er . . . I'm feeling right tired just now,' he yawned –

and much to John Christopher's sorrow,

Willie Worm crawled back under his stone, and said vaguely:

'I'll p'raps introduce you – tomorrow.'

Poor John Christopher! He were right sad – for he knew

there were worms, now, he'd never be friends with.

Because Willie wouldn't do what he were asked!

And so our story ends with

a moral: it's this, and I hope you'll take note

(though it's especially for worms to pay heed to).

You should never go back on your word; but always

keep the promises that you've agreed to.

But especially if JC you ever should meet,

show him off to your pals without fail.

You must tell the whole garden his name, till you glow

from your nose to the tip of your tail!

Consolidation

What opportunity did Willie miss? *Why* did he miss it? *(Couldn't be bothered; wouldn't stir himself; couldn't see the point, etc.)*

One of the very first things that Jesus' disciples did after the day of Pentecost, was to tell anybody who would listen about Jesus. Today, people are still doing that – there are people in this church still doing that *(give examples)*. It doesn't have to be dramatic – it could involve writing a prayer for the church magazine, visiting a family bringing a baby for infant baptism, welcoming people at a wedding, someone delivering a handout from the church around the parish *(add your own examples)*.

Focus on the particular missionary group you have chosen – these people are bothering today.

Prayer

Father God,

Jesus was the only one who was good enough

to pay the price of our sin.

Help us to spread the good news of Jesus

in whatever way you have planned for us,

and may we do this special work with enthusiasm.

In the name of Jesus.

Amen.

Prayer

Father God,

The Ladder of Life

Summary   Learning to make our choices to follow Jesus' way.

Aim   To remember that only Jesus can say: 'I am the way, the truth and the life . . . No one can come to the Father except by me.' And to recognise that the pathways the world offers us are false, and that the only way to travel is the way of Jesus.

Materials   ● Copies of sketch script.

● Props and costumes mentioned in the sketch.

Presentation

You can use this sketch without comment, because it speaks for itself. If you need an introduction, you could 'warm up' the congregation by:

(a) Saying how badly let down you were last week by your horoscope. It said you would make new friends, come unexpectedly upon some money and receive good news through the post. What actually happened was that you had a row with your neighbour about the height of his hedge; you lost a £20 note somewhere between home and the shops; and the postman delivered a letter from the Inland Revenue saying you owed £500 in back tax! Talk about the dangers of trusting in the stars and horoscopes.

(b) Can the congregation think of advice they were given which proved to be a total waste of time, or which let them down badly?

Here's a sketch that will help us as we make big decisions:

(Enter Joe Everyman. He is dressed very simply; if possible, his face should be covered by a white mask, demonstrating his anonymity. He stands next to a stepladder, which is positioned in the centre of the acting area.)

Narrator   This is Joe. Joe Everyman. He's an ordinary sort of person. He has an ordinary sort of job, lives in an ordinary kind of house in a fairly ordinary street; he drives a car. There's nothing special about it. It's quite ordinary, really. He has a wife and two children. He's a bit like a lot of other people, I suppose. You know – ordinary.

Now, you may have noticed that Joe is standing next to something. It's something very special. It's called the Ladder of Life. Joe would love to climb up the Ladder of Life to see what's at the top, but I'm afraid he can't.

He can't, because he spends most of his time running – just to keep still. Sometimes, he even runs backwards when life gets a bit difficult. And only just occasionally does he manage to take three steps forward and only one step back. I guess a lot of people here this morning know that feeling!

What Joe Everyman needs in life is a friend. Someone who will help him to climb up the Ladder of Life.

(Enter Nick De'Ath)

Nick   . . . And that's where I come in. Morning, Mr Everyman. My name's De'Ath. Nick De'Ath. Very pleased to meet you, I'm sure! So – you're having trouble climbing the old Ladder of Life, are you? Well, you won't be the first, and I'm sure you won't be the last. Now the good news is that I've come all the way from . . . from somewhere 'down under' . . . to give you the help you need!

I've come to offer you this envelope, Joe. Lovely, isn't it? It's yours for the taking . . . and inside you'll find everything you need to climb this Ladder of Life. In fact, if you use what's inside this envelope to get you to the top, you'll not just be climbing the Ladder of Life. No, that's boring and ordinary, that is. No, you'll be climbing the Ladder of Success!

(Just as Joe is about to take the envelope, a Clown comes on and blows a hooter. If the building has a balcony, let the Clown work from there.)

Clown   Hey, Joe! Don't do that! Don't touch that envelope, whatever you do. *(To the Congregation)* Morning, boys and girls!

(Clown comes into the main part of the church, shaking hands, tickling old ladies, blowing the hooter, etc.)

Nick   Oh no! It's Happy the Clown! That's not his real name, of course. His real name is Mr H. S. Pirit – Mr H. S. Pirit.

Clown   *(Eventually)* Don't take that envelope he's offering, Mr Everyman. It's all a big trick! Take this envelope, instead. This is the one you need. Everything you need to climb the Ladder of Life is in this envelope!

(Joe Everyman hovers and finally chooses Nick's envelope, which is the larger of the two.)

Nick   Very wise choice, Mr Everyman. You won't regret it. I knew you were a man who knows his own mind, as soon as I saw you. Let's see what's inside!

(Envelope contains words written on cards, attached to smallish bags of sand. As each one is mentioned, it is put round Joe's neck, or thrust into his hands, so that eventually he is so weighed down that he can hardly walk, let alone climb the ladder. Promises in envelope: cheque for £100,000; ownership of a nice house in the country; a large and expensive car; a holiday home on the coast; your own business; an expensive holiday abroad.)

Clown   Well Joe, I did try to warn you. All that glisters is not gold, you know. Feel like trying my envelope, now? You still can, if you want to – it isn't too late.

(Everyman is so weighed down he can't take the envelope. Clown opens it for him. It contains a pair of scissors, with Jesus' name attached. Clown cuts away all the clutter of Nick's 'presents' and takes the other things away from him.)

Now, I said I'd help you up the Ladder of Life, and so I will! Try these, and see if they will help carry you up!

(Clown produces balloons from out of a black plastic sack,

with words on them: LOVE, JOY, PEACE, PATIENCE, KINDNESS, GOODNESS, FAITHFULNESS, HUMILITY, SELF-CONTROL.)

(Everyman climbs up the steps, and finds something on one of the steps.)

Clown   What's that you've found? *(Joe lifts high a cross that is large enough to be seen at the back of the venue. Joe continues to the top, where there is a placard.)* What's at the top of the ladder, Joe?

(Everyman displays a placard, clearly bearing the words, ETERNAL LIFE.)

The cast freeze, and then break.

Consolidation

There are many temptations in the world, but they weigh us down and make us take our eyes off heaven. Jesus will equip us with all the gifts we need, if we ask him, so that we can walk in his way and come at last to eternal life.

Prayer

Father God,

we thank you for those people we meet in our lives who point us to you.

We thank you for Jesus, and for the gifts he gives us –

especially the promise of the gift of eternal life.

Amen.

Holidays!

Summary

Help is always there for us from the Holy Spirit, but we sometimes don't ask for it.

Aim

To remember that God has given us Jesus to help us make a perfect plan for our lives.

Materials

- An overhead transparency showing a map of IFEL ISLAND, or a very large map mounted – if possible – on a display board. The island should show all the things mentioned in the story. The landing site is on the eastern side of the south coast, and SELF ISLAND near to it. The motorway should be drawn according to the system on most British maps, and be quite short. Cut out the places mentioned in different coloured card, and stick them onto the map to make them stand out. For instance, the mountain could be cut out of holographic silver card; Hope Castle out of gold card, with black, felt-tipped edges. The main thing is that the various places on the map (which should be clearly labelled) can be easily seen from the back of the congregation. If there is any doubt about this, you could reproduce the map on the back of the service order sheet, if there is one.

- Crosses *(cut out of red card)* and ticks *(green card)* which can be stuck, with double-sided tape, onto the map. At each different location, decide whether the experience Jane had there was good or bad. If good, place a tick, if bad, a cross.

- Anything to suggest a holiday atmosphere. If you have a stage or platform, use this to mount a garden umbrella; sombrero with a pair of sunglasses around its top; cricket bat; sun cream; suitcase; fishing rod, etc. Anything to suggest colour and excitement. You could have a puppet of Cosmo the monkey *(a character in the sketch)* draped over the map board at the beginning, to give a talking point as the children arrive.

Presentation

Where would you like to go?

Somewhere you've never been?

The land of ice and snow?

Or down in a submarine?

Places far away, Siam, Madrid or Perth?

Well if you insist, at the top of the list

is a journey to the centre of the earth!

Invite the children out to the front and ask who has been on holiday. Where did you go? Who did you go with? What was the weather/place like? Did you like the food? Would you go again? What did you like best/least? If abroad, did you learn any of the language?

(If time allows, ask for a few phrases in foreign languages that might be helpful on holiday – here are a few helpful phrases in case these countries are mentioned.)

E pericoloso sporgersi *(gersi as in jersey)*
Italian: It is dangerous to lean out (of the window)!!

Tschüs!
German: *(colloquial)* Goodbye.

Yassas!
Greek: Hello.

Yassas!
Greek: Goodbye!

Are you going on holiday? Where are you going? How will you get there? Have you been before? Who's going with you? What are you looking forward to most? . . . etc.

In a moment, we shall hear a story about holidays. But in the story we will need some sound effects. Are you any good at doing these? Let's have a practice! *(Produce all the sound effects needed for the story – (a) to rehearse, and (b) to whet their appetites for what is to come.)*

Ifel Island

I know some children called Tom, Sarah and Jane who have just come back from their holiday on IFEL ISLAND. *(Pick some of the children to be the characters.)*

If you were to travel east of the sun and west of the moon, and to turn sharp right when you come to the north wind, sooner or later you will arrive at Ifel Island. Here are Tom and Jane and Sarah. They've just come back from a holiday on Ifel Island.

Their boat reached the south coast on a sunny summer afternoon. They went ashore, and were fascinated by the noise being made by the cicadas. *(Sound cue)*

'Let's get on our coach and go to our hotel on Paradise Beach. I've seen pictures of it in the brochure. It's wonderful!' said Tom. Sarah agreed, but Jane said: 'But there's already a beach *here*. I want to stay and play on it for a bit. You two catch the coach. I'll meet up with you later.'

So Tom and Sarah scratched their heads and got on the coach, leaving Jane behind to play on the beach. She had a lovely afternoon, but suddenly found the beach being covered with seawater. The tide was coming in and covering the sand. She screamed with fear, and ran as fast as she could towards SELF ISLAND *(Footsteps)*

When she had reached SELF ISLAND she felt very pleased with herself. She saw the notice and read, SELF ISLAND, and said: 'This place is called SELF ISLAND. Right! I shall please myself, and do just what I want.' She walked right round the island, giving names to all the different parts, and suddenly it grew very dark. 'Oh dear,' she said sadly. 'It's getting dark, and there's nowhere to sleep, and nothing to eat, and here I am – all by my-SELF!' She sat down on the grass. 'If only I had gone on the coach with the others,' she wailed. 'What a fool I am!' *(Crying)*

Suddenly, she heard a voice. 'Don't get upset,' said the voice. 'Sleep over there under that tree. It's nice and comfy. Tomorrow, I shall show you a tree whose fruit you can eat, and I will make you a canoe so you can row back to Ifel Island.'

'Who is it?' called Jane. But the voice had gone.

Next morning, she woke up to find a monkey hopping about beside her. He said his name was Cosmo, and if she did everything he told her, she would get back to her friends. He gave her some breakfast, and showed her the canoe – for his was the voice of the night before. They rowed ashore, and Cosmo said, 'Now we need to head for the main road.'

'Look at that!' said Jane, suddenly, and pointed to a swamp beside the path. 'What an interesting place. I bet there are all sorts of interesting things in that swamp. Let's go and explore!'

Cosmo started to protest, but Jane was off. And suddenly, she was up to her knees in mud. She cried aloud when she found she couldn't move. Suddenly she heard a very strange sound.

'What's that noise?' she squealed.

'That,' said Cosmo, 'is the sound of the marsh snakes. They're deadly poisonous. Listen. There must be about ten of them!' *(Hissing)*

'What am I going to do?' cried Jane.

'You should have taken my advice,' said Cosmo. 'Now reach out and catch hold of my hand, and I'll pull you out.'

She did what he told her, and soon she was back on dry land again.

'Now come this way,' said Cosmo, almost crossly, pulling her by the hand. But Jane had other ideas. 'I'm so tired,' she said. 'I think I'll go into that forest over there and have a short nap under one of the trees.'

'But the Wild Wood is dangerous!' said Cosmo. 'There are all sorts of nasties lurking in there!' But Jane had gone. And in five minutes she was fast asleep under a big old oak tree. But she wasn't alone. For she'd only had her eyes shut for half an hour when she was suddenly awoken by a roaring sound. A roaring sound that was getting nearer and nearer and nearer! *(Roaring)*

'That's torn it!' said Cosmo. 'There are bears in this wood . . . and they know you have invaded their territory, and they don't seem very pleased about it. We shall have to run for our lives!' And he grabbed her hand and ran out of the wood with her as fast as his little legs could carry him.

They stopped to catch their breath by a very old bridge over a river. Beside the bridge sat a very old man on a brightly coloured wooden box. He said he was the bridge keeper.

'We must cross the bridge,' said Cosmo. 'We must walk up the river, and the only path is on the other side.'

'Very well,' agreed Jane. 'Wait! Cosmo . . . what's that horrible noise?'

It was the noise of the wind . . . of a very strong and violent wind that began to blow very suddenly from the east. *(Wind)*

'There's going to be a terrible storm,' said the old man. Sure enough, the rain came battering down, just at that minute, and the ancient bridge started wobbling about in the wind.

'Never mind the storm,' shouted Cosmo, above the din of the wind, 'we have to get across the bridge.'

'I will hold the bridge steady for you,' said the old man. 'I know I look old and feeble, but will you have faith in me to keep the bridge steady and safe while you cross?'

Jane looked at him, and suddenly said: 'Yes . . . I know you can do it. Goodbye, and thank you.'

The two of them crossed the bridge in safety, and the old man hung on to the ropes for all he was worth. As soon as they reached the other side, the storm went away, just as suddenly as it had come.

Cosmo and Jane had a lovely stroll up the River of Dreams, until they came at last to a big castle.

'That is Hope Castle,' said Cosmo. 'We can be sure of a bed for the night, there. The castle keeper is a very kind old woman, and she will take us in and give us something to eat, and we shall be safe.'

And so they were. They woke bright and early, and the old woman gave them some sandwiches for the journey, and off they went towards the Narrow Way.

'Now, don't wander off the path, here,' warned Cosmo. 'This is dangerous country, and there are lots of nasties lurking in the hedges. Hold on to my tail and don't let go.'

'Oh, but what about the caves?' asked Jane. 'I've just seen a signpost down a side path pointing to the Black Caves. Do let's go and explore them.'

'Now, I don't think that is a good idea,' said Cosmo. . . . But Jane had gone. He called after her down the dark side path . . . but she had gone, running on ahead, full of excitement.

He found her an hour later, hiding at the back of one of the caves, tears streaming down her face.

'You didn't tell me there were wolves in these caves,' she spluttered. 'They chased me into this cave, and I didn't think I would ever get out of here alive. Listen. . . . Can you hear them . . .? They're still out there!' *(Howling)*

Now, Cosmo was quite cross with Jane but he said nothing to her and struck a match and lit a small fire. He took a large dead branch that was lying nearby and set light to it. 'Come with me, Jane!' he said. 'This will frighten the wolves. It will burn until we get back to the Narrow Way.' Well, Cosmo was right, for so it did. They reached the Narrow Way, and in no time at all they had arrived at Paradise Beach, where Jane's friends were so glad to see her again, they gave her three cheers. *(Three cheers for Jane)*

'It was all my own fault,' admitted Jane. 'Every time I want my own way, I land in a terrible mess. Fortunately, this time, I had Cosmo to guide me, and the old man and the old woman to help me. You won't ever go away and leave me on my own, Cosmo, will you?'

'Since you ask,' said Cosmo, gently, 'I shall stay and be your friend for ever.' And as far as I know, they are still good friends to this very day, and Jane never does anything without consulting Cosmo first!

Consolidation

Life is rather like the island of IFEL. In fact, rearrange the letters, and you have the word, LIFE (Stick this word on a card, over the word IFEL). Talk about how we often go our own way and don't pay any attention to advice offered, especially advice offered by God. If we let God in, he will lead us in the right places, even when times are difficult. But we have to invite him in. We also have to have faith that he *will* help us. Do you remember that Jane had faith that the old man would be able to hold the bridge steady? Sometimes, when we are crossing through difficult times, we need to believe that God has his hands on the bridge, as it were, and will see us through.

Bible reading: John 14:6. It might be helpful to read this before and after the talk. When dealing with very small children, I have often read a bit more of this part of John's gospel, although I have paraphrased slightly to help their understanding.

Prayer

Dear Father God,

we thank you that on our journey through life, you want to be with us,

and that you send Jesus to help us, and your Spirit to guide us.

Help us to believe and trust in you,

and be ready to ask you for your help, every day.

This we ask in the name of the living Lord Jesus.

Amen.

Family Fortunes

Summary

Relationships don't just happen. We need to work at them – especially our relationship with God.

Aim

To remember how important it is to communicate with one another, and to communicate with God.

Presentation

Perform the play.

Narrator Good evening, everyone, and welcome to another edition of *Through the Keyhole*! Tonight, we're going to look through the keyhole of an ordinary house, in an ordinary street, at an oh-so-ordinary family. Come with me, if you will, to 61 Sebastopol Street, and let's eavesdrop awhile on the Platt family . . . It's just after six o'clock on a Monday night, and here we have our Darren.

(Enter Darren. Sits in chair, watches TV)

And look! There's Grandad, back from his occupational therapy class at the community centre.

(Enter Grandad)

Grandad Is that you, our Darren?

Darren Huh!

Grandad That's the last time they get me down that community centre on a Monday! That Mrs Blodgett's a sandwich short of the full lunchbox.

Darren *(Without interest)* Oh yeah?

Grandad As soon as I got through them double doors she pounced on me! 'What are we going to do today then, Herbert? Would we like to knit a nice woolly egg cosy, or shall we settle for a lovely raffia mat?'

Darren Two sugars in mine, Grandad . . . an' I'll have one of them chocolate biscuits.

Grandad I said: 'Are you talking to me, my good woman? I'll have you know I was wounded on the podium at Dunkirk!'

Darren	It's a rubbish place. The ferry landed us there when we went up to France with the school. It was rainin'.
Grandad	I told her what to do with her egg cosies and her flippin' raffia mats, and I spent the afternoon playing dominoes with my mate, Fred.
Darren	They can't even spell it proper. They spell it with a Q-U-E, instead of with a K. That's Froggy language for you.
Grandad	Fred's wife Ethel's got a bad chest. She can't get her breath proper. He can't do nowt with her, and the doctor's worse than useless.
Darren	They tried to teach us that Froggie language at school. They wanted me to do an exam in it. Do you know what I said to 'em?
Grandad	Phosgene! That's what I said to Fred. Phosgene! Two spoonfuls of Phosgene.
	(Enter Mum, with two bags of shopping)
Mum	Haven't you set the table, our Darren?
Grandad	'You have heard of Dunkirk, I suppose, Mrs Blodgett?' I said. That made her sit up a bit, it did!
Darren	Can you turn the sound up on the telly for me, Mum? I can't hear the football results.
Mum	Darren! If you knew the sort of day I've had!
Grandad	Egg cosies! What the flippin' 'eck do I want with egg cosies?
Mum	Have you had a nice day, Grandad? How was the occupational therapy?
Grandad	Our Darren don't know he's born. When I was his age, I was working down the coal mine! Phosgene! That's the answer to her problem.

Mum   Will somebody put the kettle on?

Darren   Can you lend me a tenner, Mom? I'm goin' bowlin' at seven with me mates.

Mum   Now listen, you two! I've got something very serious to tell you.

Grandad   Egg cosies and raffia mats! Can you imagine? She's got a face like a perishin' egg cosy, 'as that Mrs Blodgett . . .

Mum   I . . . I just want you both to know that I'm leaving. In a few minutes, a Rolls-Royce will roll up outside the house. I shall take two hastily-packed suitcases and that hold-all with the leather handles that your dad couldn't carry when he left – and be whisked off down the motorway to the airport.

Darren   Oh, nice one.

Grandad   Phosgene, our Darren. Your nan swore by it.

Mum   When I get to the airport, I shall be flown out on a specially hired jet to the island of Mustique in the Caribbean, where I shall spend the rest of my live. Arnold Schwarzenegger has kindly invited me to join him in his hideaway there, and I have accepted. And when I get to my Caribbean hideaway, I'm afraid I shan't give 61 Sebastopol Street, or either of you, a second thought. Ever!

Darren   Mam – do us a favour.

Mum   What is it?

Darren   Try to get Schwarzenegger's autograph for our Davina, will you?

Mum   Ooooh!

Davina   *(Entering, with a bag of chips)* Mum – have we got any sauce?

Mum   *(Sinking into a chair)* I DON'T believe it!!

Consolidation

1. Talk about what was wrong with the relationships in the sketch. Nobody was really listening to anybody. Why did Mum make up her fanciful story? Did she really want to leave?

2. Is there a difference between hearing and listening?

3. Is there such a thing as hearing only what we want to hear? What causes us to want to do that?

What would have been Jesus' attitude to the people in the sketch? Would he have been sensitive to their individual needs, or would he have been living in a world of his own, like Darren and Grandad, totally closed off from those around him?

Can you think of any examples from the life of Jesus where he really listened to what people said to him, and did something positive in response? *(Any of the healing miracles, where people actually came and asked for him to intervene. The scene in John 14, where he heard what Thomas was saying, and was ready with an answer about the future.)*

Jesus doesn't live in a world of his own. He hears and he always – yes, always – responds. The trouble is, we so often forget or neglect to ask! In the week ahead, let's do our best to *ask* Jesus into our lives and to take control of the things in our lives – especially the difficult things, knowing that when we *ask,* he always answers. Interestingly, Jesus *asked* his Father God to help him on many occasions – he called the asking *prayer,* and we should do the same. *(Read from the Gospels the episode in the Garden of Gethsemane when Jesus prayed earnestly to the Father.)* All we have to do is ask – and then wait for God's answer!

Prayer

Father God,

in a world that doesn't listen to itself,

we would ask that you would equip us to listen to you,

and to ask you to step into our lives and the lives of those we love,

to make a difference.

We thank you for the example of Jesus, and for his prayerfulness.

Help us to take prayer seriously, and not to be afraid to *ask*,

for ourselves as well as for others. Amen.